Walt Whitman's Concept
of the
American Common Man

by

LEADIE M. CLARK

PHILOSOPHICAL LIBRARY
New York

DEDICATED TO

Leadie A. Clark

and

John T. Flanagan

Table of Contents

Introduction

SCHOLARS WHO HAVE studied Walt Whitman and his
relationship to his own time have, in many instances,
used descriptive or explanatory terms which Whitman
himself employed. Whitman spoke of himself as the
poet of democracy and the poet of the common man;
he considered himself a representative democrat. To
use these established terms simplifies considerably the
task of anyone who wishes to define the general impression left by Whitman and his works, but in a sense
these terms have lost specific meaning chiefly because
of their widespread and indiscriminate use. In many
instances, the effect was that which Whitman personally encouraged, and the various essays in Whitman
biography and interpretation have often been primarily
a continuation of the Whitman autobiography. The
robust expansiveness of *Leaves of Grass* and the pro-
phetic utterances of a dawning new day have been
taken as indicative of the general tenor and purpose of
Whitman the man and the poet.

In the preface to *The Uncollected Poetry and Prose
of Walt Whitman,* Emory Holloway remarked that
many believed that Whitman would not have been
pleased with his work, but Holloway recognized the
need for a full Whitman biography as well as autobiography. It is only through Whitman biography and
Whitman analysis that the poet's meaning will become
clear since Whitman never satisfactorily defined either

his meanings or his terms. It is characteristic of his philosophy that its effect was to be general and its chief influence on the future. But if the true meanings of his works are to be gathered, Whitman biography must supply the material necessary for specifically defining Whitman's seemingly all-inclusive terms. To achieve this end, the editorial work of various Whitman scholars must be carefully scrutinized. Works like *The Uncollected Poetry and Prose of Walt Whitman* edited by Holloway, *I Sit and Look Out* edited by Holloway and Schwartz, *New York Dissected* edited by Holloway and Adimari, *Walt Whitman of the New York Aurora* edited by Rubin and Brown, *Walt Whitman's Backward Glances* edited by Bradley and Stevenson, *Faint Clews & Indirections* edited by Gohdes and Silver, as well as the earlier *Gathering of the Forces* edited by Rodgers and Black, provide much of the material needed to discover Whitman's meanings.

Early Whitman biography had stressed the personality and appearance of the man and his work in and around Washington. The loyalty of friends, the difficulties encountered with the various editions of *Leaves of Grass,* and Whitman's general serenity and democracy were thoroughly discussed. But these works supplied the Whitman student with little knowledge of Whitman's relationship to his own age. Even Horace Traubel's voluminous *With Walt Whitman in Camden* revealed a paucity of ideas and a tendency to moralize. More recent works like Alice Lovelace Cook's *Whitman's Backgrounds in the Life and Thought of his Times* and Hargis Westerfield's *Walt Whitman's Reading,* an unpublished doctoral dissertation at Indiana University, show that Whitman knew no more of his age generally than the common American man did. Although he began his literary career as a journalist, he was not deeply influenced by the movements of his own day. He was widely rather than deeply read. He voiced in his journalistic writings the views of the average common man at the same time that he was offering to the world his theory of spiritual democracy in *Leaves of Grass*. After 1855, he concerned himself with both prose and verse, editing various newspapers until 1860, and supervising the editions of *Leaves of Grass*. He thought he saw the fruition of his dreams for the common man during the Civil War. *Drum-Taps* was the result. But the true nature of the Reconstruction period escaped him, and Whitman retired to his dreams of spiritual democracy and the future common man.

His disgust with his own age and his dreams for the future formed the subject matter of his essay, *Democratic Vistas*. After 1871, prose became more and more the medium for Whitman, and the works *Specimen Days and Collect, November Boughs,* and *Goodbye, My Fancy* were primarily prose pieces. Whitman had added all that he could to his poetic message of spiritual democracy after he included *Drum-Taps* in *Leaves of Grass*.

The term "poet of democracy" has been analyzed most recently by Hugh I'Anson Fausset in his book *Walt Whitman: Poet of Democracy*. Numerous biographers have dealt with Whitman's democracy and his role as a representative democrat, but little has been done with Whitman's concept of the common man. It has been assumed that Whitman's common man was all-inclusive and that his assertion that *Leaves of Grass* was directed to and written for the common man, included men the world over as well as all Americans.

It is the purpose of this book to clarify, as far as possible, what Whitman meant by the expression "the American common man." It would appear that since America recognizes no established and hereditary aristocracy, Whitman's sweeping surveys of American occupations included all American men and women. These men and women, because they were American, could become heroes in whatever trade or occupation they pursued. To test the theory of Whitman's all-inclusiveness, one must sift his prose writings as well as his poetry to discover what Whitman himself specifically wrote on the common man and on various groups of people who help make up America's heterogeneous population. I shall not defend or refute Whitman's universality, but rather define the term "the common man" and illustrate its effect on Whitman generalizations. For this reason, I have given a great deal of attention to quotations from the works of Whitman. Often these quotations are long and detailed, but two dangers had to be avoided. The first of these is the appearance that certain key utterances of Whitman had been made to support a particular thesis through the use of ellipsis, and the second is that a thesis was being supported with flimsy and scanty evidence cleverly used. Hence, I have tried to show the consistency of Whitman's thought from the beginning of his journalistic career to the publication of *Specimen Days and Collect* and *November Boughs*. It is only through a careful study of Whitman's various prose writings that one can truly learn what he meant by the common man and the divine average. A further attempt has been made to distinguish clearly between Whitman's romantic utterances and his realistic ones, for it is the realistic utterances which determine to what extent Whitman can be considered a representative democrat. In short, although Whitman did not specifically define the common man, such a definition is inherent in his works and this work is a search for clues to the definition. The search has been as exhaustive as possible. The findings are duly recorded.

Because of the painstaking research of various Whitman scholars, there are today no significant gaps in the Whitman biography, and it is probably safe to say that few of his extant writings have escaped being discovered and collected. *Leaves of Grass* has been interpreted and reinterpreted and various prose pieces have been used to illustrate various aspects of Whitman's developing philosophy. Through the aid of his journalistic writings, Whitman's awareness of his own age and his attitude toward social, political, and intellectual movements have been explored. The first chapter of this book shows Whitman's relation to his own age as revealed through his editorials and other prose pieces. The second chapter is a detailed analysis of his expressed attitude toward various groups of people and his general concept of the native American man. The third chapter explores Whitman's concept of the common man of the future and the function the poet must perform in shaping that common man. The fourth chapter investigates Whitman's right to be called a representative democrat in the light of newly amassed evidence. The fifth chapter summarizes the material previously presented.

Obviously this book could not have been written if Whitman scholars had not already collected and republished the early works of Whitman. The recent work of Rubin and Brown and of Gohdes and Silver has been of inestimable value. Because of the labors of these scholars, it is now easier to divorce the Whitman myth from Whitman the man and the poet.

Biographical Outline

1819   Born at West Hills, New York.

1823   Whitman family moved to Brooklyn.

1832   Wrote verses for the *Long Island Patriot*.

1832–36 Learned the trade of printing.

1836–1840–1 In the country as a teacher and newspaperman.

1838   At Huntington where he founded a weekly journal, the *Long Islander*.

1841   Entered the office of the *New World* as a compositor. "Death in the Schoolroom," poetry and other stories submitted to the *New World* and the *Democratic Review*.

1842   *Franklin Evans, or The Inebriate*. Wrote for the *New York Sun*, acted as editor of the *Aurora* and later of the *Tattler*.

1843   Editor of the *Statesman*.

1844   Editor of the *Democrat* while contributing also to the *Columbian Magazine*, the *American Review*, and Poe's *Broadway Journal*.

1843 or 1844 Contributed political poems to Horace Greeley's *Tribune*.

1845   Worked for the Brooklyn *Star*.

1846   Editor of the Brooklyn *Daily Eagle*. Supported the Mexican War.

1848   Left the *Eagle* after a split in the Democratic Party. Whitman was a "Barnburner" or Free Soil Democrat. To New Orleans for three months and a problematical romance. Traveled through the country on the trip to and from New Orleans. Returned to Brooklyn and established the *Freeman*.

Early 1850's Worked as a carpenter.

1850   Contributed to the *Brooklyn Advertiser*.

1855   Gave up carpentering. Published *Leaves of Grass* containing a preface and twelve poems. Received the praise of Emerson in a letter dated July 21, 1855.

1856   Second edition of *Leaves of Grass* containing several new poems which later formed the nucleus of the "Children of Adam." Emerson's letter was also printed.

1855–6   Wrote for *Life Illustrated*. Wrote but did not print "Eighteenth Presidency."

1857–8   Studied oratory and making notes for addresses.

1857–61   Frequenter of Pfaff's German restaurant.

1857–59   Editor of Brooklyn *Daily Times*.

1860   Boston edition of *Leaves of Grass* by Thayer and Elridge which included the "Children of Adam" and "Calamus" poems.

1860–1   Wrote sketches on New York hospitals and Brooklyn.

1862   Went to Washington and to battlefields looking for wounded brother, George.

1862–6   Worked in hospitals of Washington. Wrote for New York papers.

1864   First serious illness. Went home to Brooklyn. Finished *Drum-Taps*.

1865   *Drum-Taps* published. Recalled on death of Lincoln and poem "When Lilacs Last in the Dooryard Bloom'd" added.

1865   Obtained clerkship in Indian Bureau of the Department of Interior. Dismissed as an immoral poet. O'Connor wrote *The Good Gray Poet* for which Whitman suggested the title. Transferred to the Attorney-General's Office. Friendship with Peter Doyle.

1867   New edition of *Leaves of Grass*. Critical recognition in England. Issued "Notes on Walt Whitman as Poet and Person."

1868   Selections from *Leaves of Grass* appeared in England under D. G. Rossetti's sponsorship.

1871   Editions of *Leaves of Grass* including *Drum-Taps, Democratic Vistas,* and *Passage to India.* Gave his "Song of the Exposition" at the opening of the annual exhibition of the American Institute.

1872   Recited "As a Strong Bird on Pinions Free" at Dartmouth College. Poem also published.

1873   Whitman's really serious paralytic stroke. Death of his mother. Moved to his brother's in Camden.

1875   English and Irish subscription raised for Whitman.

1876–82 Visits to Timber Creek and its vicinity which furnished material for *Specimen Days.*

1876   Centennial edition of *Leaves of Grass. Two Rivulets.*

1878   Delivered lecture "Death of Lincoln" in Steck Hall, New York. Tour of sixteen weeks across the country.

1881   Lecture "Death of Lincoln" given in Boston. Osgood edition of *Leaves of Grass* and attack urged by the Society for the Suppression of Vice. Ultimate discontinuance of the edition.

1882   Edition taken over by David McKay. Published *Specimen Days and Collect.*

1884   Purchased and moved into the house on Mickle Street.

1886   Second English subscription.

1888   Published *November Boughs* which contained the essay "A Backward Glance O'er Travel'd

Roads." Steadily declining health. Camden edition of *Complete Poems and Prose.*

1889   Birthday edition of *Leaves of Grass.*

1891   Published *Goodbye, My Fancy.* Whitman busy with the building of his tomb.

1892   Whitman died. *Complete Prose Works* issued.

CHAPTER I

Whitman and His Age

THE INTEREST of American literary figures in things American during the period from 1830 to the Civil War and after cannot be compared to the "Young German" movement, but it revealed, nevertheless, that America's intellectual leaders had not divorced themselves from the age in which they lived. As a group, they generally recognized the problems with which the new democracy was faced. Writers like Emerson, Thoreau, Channing, and Alcott expressed themselves on social and political happenings even if only in their diaries. These men were interested in the destiny of man, and though they did work for man's social and economic advancement, they were more interested in the individual's complete self-development. Thus, the programs they offered for the development of man were best suited for the individual and not the group.

Since Walt Whitman began his literary career as a journalist, he found himself a privileged commentator on the political, economic, and social scene. As editor of the *Aurora* (1841-5), the Brooklyn *Eagle* (1846-7), the *Freeman* (1848-9), the Brooklyn *Times* (1857-9), the *Tattler,* the *Statesman,* and the *Democrat,* each for brief periods, and as a contributor to various other newspapers, Whitman expressed his views on many of the movements of his day. He showed himself to be

1

antagonistic toward some and a follower of others. He began his journalistic career about the time of the organization of the Whig Party. A strong anti-Jackson group had grown up which included those who resented the Jacksonian attacks on monopoly and on the United States Bank, those who were hostile to the growing foreign population and believed that all the naturalized citizens belonged to the Democratic Party, and those who objected to the methods Jackson had used in handling the nullification controversy. However, Jacksonian democracy was still all-pervasive. The Jacksonians had tended to exalt human rights as a counterweight to property rights. Hence, the Jacksonian tendency was a leveling tendency since it was to be assumed that the human rights of each man were equal and that an equitable distribution of the wealth of the country would render all men equal. Jacksonians moderated that side of Jeffersonianism which talked of agricultural virtue, independent proprietors, "natural property," and the abolition of industrialism, and expanded that side of Jeffersonianism which talked of economic equality, the laboring classes, human rights, and the control of industrialism.[1] In preference to Jefferson's agrarian philosophy, Jacksonians adopted Adam Smith's labor theory of value. They believed in the equitable distribution of property, battled against the concentration of wealth and power in a single class, and demanded the opening up of western lands. Jacksonians were for hard money and gradually reduced the paper circulation in an effort to eliminate all notes under twenty dollars. The writings of Jackson offer no clear-cut exposition of what might be labeled the Jacksonian theory of

[1] Arthur M. Schlesinger, Jr., *The Age of Jackson* (Boston, 1947), p. 312.

democracy, but laissez-faire, the rights of the common man, and the rights of labor were integral parts of his doctrine. The American economic theorists who held theories favorable to the development of Jacksonianism were Gouge, Leggett, Sedgwick, and Cambreleng, all of whom expounded the antimonopolistic traditions formulated by Adam Smith, as well as G. H. Evans, Ely Moore, and John Ferral, who expounded the pro-labor doctrine of William Cobbett.[2]

William Gouge was a former editor of a Jackson newspaper and a Treasury official who was interested, primarily, in preventing the establishment of new banks, particularly in rural areas. He argued that if bank notes were eliminated, enough specie would circulate to supply the needs of trade; responsible private bankers would perform all necessary banking functions. He also argued that a bimetallic standard was an absurdity since no law could fix the value between the two metals.[3] William Leggett, the first public leader of the Loco-Focos, sought to free the laboring class from the oppression of aristocratic-minded monopolists. He bitterly opposed a measure to forbid the use of credit in stock-exchange operations and informed the South in 1835 that the members of the Democratic Party in the North supported the southern slave policy to protect themselves from the threat of competition from free Negro labor.[4] Theodore Sedgwick proposed to better the lot of labor through education. He became a promoter of railroads and of the expansion of lower education as the means of achieving equal rights for all.

[2] *Ibid.*, pp. 307-308.
[3] Joseph Dorfman, *The Economic Mind in American Civilization, 1606-1865* (New York, 1946), p. 608.
[4] *Ibid.*, pp. 653-654.

People could raise themselves only by acquiring property, virtue, and education. He disapproved of squatters on the public lands. He believed the public lands were intended for the poorer and less fortunate people who, through industrious labor, could acquire the land cheaply.[5] Churchill C. Cambreleng had argued that bills of exchange, mortgages, and private notes of various kinds would replace bank notes. Therefore he believed that the power to issue currency should be vested in a wealthy corporation which could be closely watched and was less exposed to bankruptcy than individuals.[6] All of these men were primarily interested in financial matters and were prominent Loco-Focos.

G. H. Evans was interested in land reform. He argued that since capital was the result of labor, there could be no equal right to capital, but the soil was the gift of nature and everyone had a natural right to the soil as well as to the product of his labor. Therefore, in the abstract, land should be equally distributed, but since this could not be done directly in the settled states, the public lands should be given free to the settlers. Such a policy would cause the falling of land prices throughout the country and would begin the limiting of land ownership until eventually land values would be exclusively the improvements on the land. Inequality of land ownership would thus be eliminated.[7] Ely Moore believed that the stability of the government and the liberty of the people were being threatened by an undue accumulation and distribution of wealth. He was the first president of the General Trades Union formed in 1833 and believed that trade unions promoted

[5] *Ibid.*, pp. 651-652.
[6] *Ibid.*, p. 546.
[7] *Ibid.*, pp. 684-685.

a more healthful distribution of property, thus preserving the economic foundations of democracy.[8] John Ferral was one of the most popular labor leaders of the day and with Ely Moore directed the destiny of trade unionism.

These economists and labor leaders were all Loco-Focos. They believed that the aristocracy of money had destroyed the aristocracy of land, and that labor would destroy the aristocracy of money. They believed that the day of the common man had dawned. Whitman was, for a time, a Loco-Foco shortly after his break with the Democratic Party on the question of Free Soil. He was always an ardent Jacksonian and his newspaper, the *Freeman*, was a Free Soil organ. However, an unpublished investigation of Whitman's reading does not cite a single book in economic theory. He was, however, an avid reader of the newspaper and through that medium probably kept abreast of the prevailing economic and political writing both through news stories and through book reviews. Whitman's own statements are not to be trusted implicitly since he made, on some occasions, a deliberate effort to conceal the extent of his reading. For instance, Whitman told Hartmann in 1884 that he had never read Rousseau.[9] Yet Gohdes and Silver print a translation of a part of Rousseau's *Contrat Social* which was found in the Bucke Collection.[10] However, no date is assigned. Too, Whitman was an ardent admirer of Frances Wright, and as a newspaperman he probably "covered" numerous lectures on the economic theories of the day. Since

[8] Schlesinger, Jr., *op. cit.*, pp. 192-193.

[9] Sadakichi [Hartmann], *Conversations with Walt Whitman* (New York, 1895), p. 26.

[10] Clarence Gohdes and Rollo G. Silver, *Faint Clews & Indirections* (Durham, 1949), pp. 33-41.

there exists no concrete proof that he studied the works of any economists, modern researchers can find no proof to substantiate Binns' statement that "he was doubtless influenced by Mill, whose *Principles of Political Economy* he seems to have studied soon after its appearance in 1848."[11]

Nevertheless, though lacking background in economic theory, Whitman never hesitated to express his views on many of the issues which were of especial interest to Jacksonians. That Whitman's views were so often in conformity with Jacksonian democracy can be explained as an outgrowth of his Jeffersonianism and his devotion to "party." Until Whitman split with the Democratic Party on the question of Free Soil, he was a loyal party man, and on several occasions attempted to have his newspaper designated as the official party organ. A certain amount of Jacksonianism is obviously to be expected in his writings. For *Life Illustrated,* Whitman wrote articles on decent housing for workingmen. On numerous occasions, he expressed his views on the economic needs of the workingmen.

> The lowest possible imposts on trade, in any way—as little paper money as possible—legislatures, both general and State abstaining from meddling so much with the relation between labor and its payment, . . . these, in such a truly "great" country as ours, involve the real interests of the workingmen.[12]

Knowing little about free trade except "instinctively," he wrote,

[11] Henry B. Binns, *A Life of Walt Whitman* (London, 1905), p. 308.
[12] Cleveland Rodgers and John Black, ed., *The Gathering of the Forces,* Vol. I (New York, 1920), pp. 68-69. Hereafter referred to as *Gathering of the Forces.*

. . . We free traders are striking out in the mighty game of the world for our market, and distant kingdoms for our commercial tributaries! What is there to say us nay in this? We have, in this vast Republic, every variety of climate, soil, and production. We have the greatest staple in the world nearly altogether in our own hands. We have enterprise and physical power, and steam power, beyond all nations. — Cut us loose from the antiquated bandages of the tariff system—place us on the broad sea of freedom of trade, with the unchained wind and full sails—and we will show the world such a spectacle of solid commercial grandeur, not merely beyond all English greatness, but towering to such a stupendous height as men never before conceived or had any idea of![13]

Whitman gloried in America's industrial prospects; yet he saw no need to protect so-called infant industries by means of a tariff. Although the tariff was to divide the country sectionally on the question of economic or social expediency and the question of constitutionality, Whitman was primarily interested in neither of these questions but in who was to pay the tariff desired by some manufacturers to protect infant industries. Whitman cared nothing for Clay's American System, which proposed a manufacturing East as the market for an agricultural West. In 1842, he wrote:

A few cliques of selfish manufacturers, joined with a few sap head simpletons, are raising a great hue and cry to get up the old tariff system with a new name. We hope the American nation will not allow these hypocrites to deceive them. The whole pith and essence of their movement is *self*. Under loud mouthed demonstrations of patriotism, they would push ahead

[13] *Ibid.*, pp. 64-65.

measures for their own interest. They worship the Almighty Dollar—and to aid themselves therein, they take the name of national prosperity in vain.[14]

Whitman did not believe in a tariff for revenue or for raising funds for internal improvements. He wrote:

It would be far better, were the national expenses paid by direct taxation. These roundabout, circumlocutory ways of getting money always have more or less villainy interwoven in them.[15]

In the editorial "Who Gets the Plunder?," Whitman asserted:

It would be of some excuse and satisfaction if even a fair proportion of it went to the masses of laboring-men—resulting in homesteads to such, men, women, children—myriads of actual homes in fee simple, in every state, (not the false glamour of the stunning wealth reported in the census, in the statistics, or tables in the newspapers), but a fair division and generous average to those workmen and workwomen—*that* would be something. But the fact is nothing of the kind. The profits or "protection" go altogether to a few score select persons—who, by favors of Congress, State legislatures, the banks, and other special advantages, are forming a vulgar aristocracy, full as bad as anything in the British or European castes, of blood, or the dynasties there of the past.[16]

There can be no doubt that Whitman was a free-trader. He remained so to the end of his life but felt that

[14] J. J. Rubin and C. H. Brown, *Walt Whitman of the New York Aurora* (State College, Pa., 1950), p. 97. Hereafter referred to as *Aurora*.

[15] *Ibid.*, p. 97.

[16] Walt Whitman, *Complete Prose Works* (Boston, 1907), p. 327. Hereafter referred to as *Complete Prose*.

no man had appeared who could fully explain the doctrine, for all the exponents of free trade held to some private convictions that qualified the purity of their belief. Traubel recorded Whitman as saying:

> In this campaign it strikes me that the whole batch of the spell-binders and statesmen so-called (God help us, Statesmen!) are all wrong, all sides—discussing the problem from a vulgar point of view—poor, petty, unworthy, insincere, insulting in fact. These men never get up high enough to see what the problem in reality is—never recognize it in its international complications—do not see that it is not political but human —that it means to Bohemia as well as to America.[17]

Here is shown Whitman's desire to romanticize, to attempt a more mystical approach in solving what was essentially a completely practical problem. Whitman's spiritual view of man became entangled with his economic theory of laissez-faire. It is probable that a thorough understanding of the doctrine of laissez-faire and of the labor theory of value might have resulted in a qualification of Whitman's views of free trade in much the same manner that the views of other free traders were qualified.

But there were other aspects of the period from 1836 to 1860 which interested Whitman. The Panic of 1837 supplied the anti-Jackson Whigs with excellent political material in the 1840 presidential campaign. The Whigs blamed Jacksonian policies and Van Buren, who had been elected through Jackson's influence in 1836, for the depression. Offering no particular political platform, the Whigs selected William Henry Harrison as their candidate for president. The Whigs posed as the party

[17] Horace Traubel, *With Walt Whitman in Camden,* Vol. II (New York, 1908), p. 186.

of the people and conducted a campaign distinguished only by references to log cabins and hard cider. Harrison died in 1841 and was succeeded by his vice-president, John Tyler, an independent Democrat from Virginia, who represented a large group of Democrats who had objected to Jackson's nationalism which had revealed itself in his handling of the nullification controversy. Tyler in his message to Congress advised that the subtreasury be eliminated and its place taken by a "suitable fiscal agent," that the proceeds of the public land sales be distributed among the states to help rehabilitate their credit, and that the tariff, for the present, be let alone.[18] Clay who had expected to be the power behind the throne of the Harrison administration, offered a counter plan comprising the Whig principles which included the repeal of the independent Treasury Act and the chartering of a new United States Bank, the enactment of a protective tariff, and the distribution of the proceeds from the sales of public lands to the states for internal improvements.[19] Tyler vetoed two bank bills, allowed only a moderate tariff bill to be passed, and refused to let it be put into effect until Clay gave up his scheme for the distributing of the proceeds of public land sales to the states. Whitman's objections to the tariff and to Clay's American system have already been noted. On the question of the public lands in general, Whitman had little to say other than that he wanted those lands to stay free of slavery.

In foreign affairs, Tyler's program was definitely expansionist and imperialistic. China granted the United States the principle of extra-territoriality. The Canadian-

[18] Harold Faulkner, *American Political and Social History* (New York, 1943), pp. 298-299.
[19] *Ibid.*, 299-300.

United States border dispute was settled, and American recognition of the independence of Texas in 1837 led to friction with the Mexican government. The annexation of Texas which was supported by the slave-holding states precipitated the Mexican War during the Polk administration, and slavery again became a national issue.

At the close of the eighteenth century, slavery in America had seemed on the edge of disappearing since the institution was proving unprofitable in the South. However, the invention of the cotton gin, which made the raising of short staple cotton profitable, revitalized slavery. Since the slave trade was forbidden in all states except Georgia, the price of slaves mounted and parts of the South began agitation for the reopening of the slave trade. An institution which had been first defended as a necessary evil was now embraced and supported as a positive good sanctioned by God. Efforts were made to extend slavery into newly opened lands, and the problem became one of free labor versus slave labor. The slave uprising in Virginia in 1831 caused the passing of strenuous laws called Slave Codes, provisions of which, among other things, forbade Negroes to be absent from the plantation without written permission, forbade their being taught to read and write, and forbade their assembling without the presence of a white man.[20] In 1831, also, William Lloyd Garrison founded his newspaper, the *Liberator*, an abolitionist organ. The Underground Railroad was organized and abolitionism became a militant movement. Generally, the northern public thought of slavery as a problem of the southern people to be solved through state action.

[20] H. C. Hockett, *Political and Social Growth of the American People*, 1492-1865 (New York, 1940), p. 617.

They further believed that it was a moral issue.[21] However, after the annexation of Texas had precipitated a
war with Mexico, the question of free or slave soil
became a major political issue. The war was actually a
war of conquest designed to annex new territory. The
country was swept by a "jingo" spirit under the guise of
"manifest destiny." Although the Oregon dispute had
been peacefully settled with Great Britain, acquisitive
eyes were still cast on Canada. An attempt was made
to buy Cuba, and the question of the extension of
slavery was inextricably bound up with that of territorial expansion, resulting, therefore, in greater sec-
tional discord.

In an attempt to forestall the spread of slavery,
David Wilmot offered an amendment to the appropria-
tions bill of 1846 providing that slavery should be
prohibited in all newly acquired territory. The proviso
was defeated. The Barnburners, who wanted constitu-
tional assurance that slavery would not exist in newly
acquired territory, broke with the Democratic Party
and campaigned for free trade, free labor, free soil, free
speech, and free men. The year 1850 was marked by
the Missouri Compromise and the Fugitive Slave Act. A
lull in the free soil versus slave soil dispute resulted
from the compromise until 1854, when the old conflict
was revived by the Kansas-Nebraska Act.

During all this controversy, Whitman had his say
from time to time. In 1841, he was one of Brooklyn's
fifteen delegates to a Free-Soil Convention.[22] He wrote
a number of editorials on the question of free labor

[21] *Ibid.*, p. 622.
[22] Emory Holloway, ed., *The Uncollected Poetry and Prose of Walt
Whitman,* Vol. I (New York, 1932), p. xxxv. Hereafter referred to as
Uncollected.

versus slave labor, but attempts by Whitman scholars to defend Whitman's views on slavery call either for a partial justification of slavery as not necessarily an unmixed evil or the discussion of the problem as a purely moral one. The truth of the matter is that if Whitman had not been constantly promoting the cause of the white workingman, actual Negro slavery would have caused him few qualms, for on the question of Negro slavery he was as often pro-slavery as anti-slavery. If there had been no threat to white labor, Negro slavery would have been a moral question that would have been ultimately settled in the future. Nor can one trace a change in Whitman's point of view. His views are marked, rather, by equivocation. The really interesting factor is that most of Whitman's views on slavery are gained from works written after 1855 and that the Negro, as will be pointed out later, is only partially admitted into the universal democracy of *Leaves of Grass*.

However, in an editorial in the *Aurora* on April 2, 1842, Whitman discussed a picture contrasting the idyllic life of slaves in the South with that of an English laboring family. The purpose of the whole editorial, which was directed at the English, was as follows:

Let our transatlantic neighbors take the beam out of their own eyes—and then they can reasonably find fault with the mote in ours. Let them cease to coin the sweat, and labor, and blood, and misery of the mass, into an inflated prosperity for the few. Let them pull down the lumbering fabric of monarchy and aristocracy that has stood long enough, and too long. Let them destroy the prevalence of the spectacle of famine, penury, and death, that make Britain but one vast poor house—and then they can send us some of their charity and their sympathy.[23]

Thus, in 1842, Whitman pointed out quite graphically that compared to the British laborer, the slave laborer was idyllically happy and that consequently the problem of American slavery should concern England on no basis whatever. Here can be seen Whitman's strong sense of nationalism and native Americanism.

In 1846, Whitman did not justify slavery nor did he condemn it. The following passage could give a measure of comfort to either side.

> It is not ours to find an excuse for slaving, in the benighted condition of the African. Has not God seen fit to make him, and leave him so? Nor is it any less our fault because the chiefs of that barbarous land fight with each other, and take slave-prisoners. The whites encourage them, and afford them a market. Were that market destroyed there would soon be no supply.[24]

Here Whitman revealed his ignorance of the ways slaves were procured in Africa and considered the African benighted in his native home. Whitman barely freed himself from the charge of seeking heavenly sanction for slavery in the sentence, "Were that market destroyed, there would soon be no supply."

Much in the same vein, Whitman wrote in 1857:

> In their own country degraded, cruel, almost bestial, the victims of cruel chiefs, and of bloody rites— their lives never secure—no education, no refinement, no elevation, no political knowledge,—such is the gen-

[23] *Aurora*, p. 127.
[24] *Uncollected*, Vol. II, p. 9.

eral condition of the African tribes. From these things they are sold to the American plantation.

Would we then defend the slave trade? No; we would merely remind the reader that, in a large view of the case, the change is not one for the worse, to the victims of that trade. The blacks, mulattoes &c., either in the Northern or Southern States, might bear in mind that had their forefathers remained in Africa, and their birth occurred there, they would now be roaming Krumen or Ashanteemen wild, filthy, paganistic—not residents of a land of light, and bearing their share, to some extent, in all its civilizations.[25]

It is to be remembered that the preceding passage was written after the so-called patriarchal system of slavery had disappeared, the severe Slave Codes adopted, and the strenuous Fugitive Slave Act passed. If Whitman did not here defend the slave trade, he at least found a partial justification for it and for the existence of slavery.

A politico-economic justification can be found in these statements:

For the Brazils, for Cuba, and it may be for some of the Southern States of this Confederacy, the infusion of slaves and the prevalent use of their labor are not objectionable on politico-economic grounds. Slaves are there because they must be—when the time arrives for them not to be proper there, they will leave.[26]

Two articles, one in *New York Dissected* and the other in *I Sit and Look Out*, offer interesting studies of Whitman's attitude on the slave trade. In the first article he called for an effective course of action against so hideous a crime as engaging in the slave trade. He

[25] *Ibid.*
[26] *Ibid.*, p. 10.

described a slave ship and imagined the horrors of
the middle passage. He spoke with horror of the fact
that slavers were being fitted out in New York harbor.
Yet in 1857, in *I Sit and Look Out,* he admitted that
while the slave trade flourished it was not carried on as
vigorously as some newspapers thought. He labeled as
preposterous an assertion that the ebony line to Cuba
numbered almost three hundred ships. Whitman was
more interested, however, in the possibility that through
a continuation of the slave trade, blacks in Cuba might
become strong enough to rebel successfully. He concluded by pointing out "what a beautiful prospect is
here presented for our southern planters. A black
republic almost within sight of their shores."[27] Although
Whitman could celebrate the fight for liberty that
might be engaged in by any European revolutionary,
any threat of revolt by blacks was to be avoided. Any
rebellion on their part was something to be guarded
against constantly.

The horrors of the middle passage were, according
to Whitman, not a result of the slave trade at all. He
wrote in 1857,

> The worse results of the slave trade are those mainly
> caused by attempts of the government to outlaw it. We
> speak of the horrors of the "middle passage,"—the
> wretched, suffocating, steaming, thirsty, dying crowds
> of black men, women and children, packed between
> decks in cutter-built ships, modelled not for space, but
> speed. This, we repeat, is not an inherent attribute of
> the slave trade, but of declaring it piracy.[28]

Whitman expressed no views on what the result
would have been if the slave trade had not been

[27] Emory Holloway and Vernolian Schwartz, *I Sit and Look Out*
(New York, 1932), p. 87. Hereafter referred to as *I Sit and Look Out*.
[28] *Uncollected,* Vol. II, p. 9.

declared piracy. Holloway and others have justified Whitman's views on slavery on the basis that his grandfather held slaves, that he had spent several months in the South, and that he tried to look at both sides of an issue. However, although Whitman's editorial writings show him to be nonpartisan on very few issues, he often shows a tendency to rationalize by romanticizing, thus obscuring some evidences of partisanship. At the same time, much has been made of Whitman's anti-slavery notes published by Furness in *Walt Whitman's Workshop*. The notes are a part of the material which scholars have used to substantiate the fact that Whitman was interested in oratory.[29] For example, the notes begin:

> As of the orator advancing
> As, for example, having been engaged to deliver one of the "Lessons" to an Anti Slavery Meeting—he does not go smiling and shaking hands, waiting on the platform with the rest—but punctual to the hour, appears at the platform-steps with a friend, and ascends the platform, silent, rapid, stern, almost fierce—and delivers an oration of liberty—up-braiding, full of invective—with enthusiasm.[30]

The notes are highly romantic and not in the least abolitionist. This paragraph is illustrative:

> You have learned that the only safe law for religious sects is equal and universal toleration to all of whatever numbers, ages, hues, or language or belief.— Learn that still below this law there lies one larger and more vital to our safety, every one of us; that of the

[29] Finkel in an article, "Walt Whitman's Notes on Oratory," *American Literature*, Vol. XXII (March, 1950) has proved that Whitman's notes on oratory are not original. The notes here quoted may not be original.

[30] C. J. Furness, *Walt Whitman's Workshop* (Cambridge, 1928), p. 74.

uniform and inherent right of every man and woman to life and liberty, which as no power can take away from an innocent man without outrage, so every such person on whom that outrage is attempted has the inalienable right to defend himself.—*As to assisting such a person, it is not likely I shall ever have the privilege,* but if I can do it, whether he be black or whether he be white, whether he be an Irish fugitive or an Italian or German or Carolina fugitive, whether he come over sea or over land, if he comes to me he gets what I can do for him.—*He may be coarse, fanatical, and a nigger, he may have shown bad judgment, but while he has committed no crime further than seeking his liberty and defending it, as the Lord God liveth, I would help him and be proud of it, and protect him if I could.*—[31]

The entire paragraph, especially the last third, is provocative. Did Whitman mean to imply that it was a crime for the Negro to seek his freedom? If so, the first half and last half of this paragraph contradict each other. That he was not a true abolitionist is evident, for Whitman's attitude in this entire paragraph is one of "if I could." Needless to say, the notes were never made into a speech and delivered publicly. Whitman's true views on slavery could well have been this paragraph written in 1857:

In the meantime, it should be remembered that the institution of slavery is not at all without its redeeming points, and also that there are just as great reforms needed in the Northern States. Perhaps, there are greater reforms needed here, than in the Southern States.[32]

[31] *Ibid.*, pp. 76-77. Italics are mine.
[32] *I Sit and Look Out,* pp. 87-88.

Yet, wherever slavery touched upon the destiny of the white workingman, Whitman vigorously expressed his views. Whitman made himself the spokesman of the white workingman editorially, and sought to raise the dignity of labor. Labor was not to be sullied with the taint of slavery, but the institution of slavery debased all labor, skilled and unskilled. The South was graphic proof. In any area where slavery existed, free labor could not prosper. In 1847, Whitman wrote,

> The question whether or no there shall be slavery in the new territories which it seems conceded on all hands we are largely to get through this Mexican war, is a question between the *grand body of white workingmen, the millions of mechanics, farmers, and operatives of our country,* with their interests, on the one side—and the interests of the few thousand rich, "polished," and aristocratic owners of slaves at the south, on the other side. Experience has proved, (and the evidence is to be seen now by any one who will look at it) that a stalwart mass of respectable workingmen cannot exist, much less flourish, in a thorough slave state.[33]

Yet, Whitman was an ardent supporter of the Mexican War and heartily approved the annexation of Mexican lands. He favored the annexation of Cuba, already well stocked with slaves, and wrote:

> It is impossible to say what the future will bring forth, but "manifest destiny" certainly points to the speedy annexation of Cuba by the United States.[34]

Whitman did not realize that in supporting the Mexican War and the annexation of Cuba, he was opposing

[33] *Uncollected,* Vol. I, p. 171.
[34] *I Sit and Look Out,* p. 157.

the cause of the free white workingman. Whitman was never a deep or consistent thinker and thus failed to realize that the South favored both the war and the annexation of Cuba since the land to be acquired was suitable for the extension of slavery. Whitman lost sight of the reasons back of "manifest destiny" in his obvious joy in the mere physical expansion of the country. Many New York newspapers recognized the ultimate aims of the Mexican War and refused to support the war. Whitman took them to task for not favoring such a glorious venture.

The lands acquired by the Mexican War and the desire to preserve the Union led to the Compromise of 1850 which admitted California to the Union as a free state, adjusted the boundaries of Texas, divided the rest of the cession into two territories of Utah and New Mexico which were to be admitted as slave or free according to their constitutions, abolished the slave trade in the District of Columbia, and enacted a drastic fugitive slave law. It was the fugitive slave law that horrified most of the North and nearly all the literary men of the day.[35] Not only did the fugitive slave law drag back into captivity Negroes who had been free for years, but this was done without trial by jury. Private citizens were forced, more or less, to assist in the capture of escaped slaves. Whitman, after a brief hesitation, decided that the law must be obeyed to the letter for the good of the nation. Nothing must be allowed to disturb the bond of union among the states and the union must be preserved at all costs. His attitude was summed up in the following editorial:

[35] Emerson, Thoreau, Lowell, and Whittier were all moved to protest against the law either publicly or privately.

The N. Y. *Sun* (24th,) says, in an article against the unity of the United States as one government: "The liberty of the country is centered in the independence of the states, and with a good understanding with each other a general government might be dispensed with. Our government is a union of free states, and not a consolidation of states." . . . Our government for certain purposes, *is* a "consolidation." The wisdom of that principle is proved in the past and present; but in the local matters of the state, this consolidation does not give congress the right to interfere.—Perhaps no human institution—from which so much clashing was expected —has ever turned out better, than the "separate independence" of the federal and state governments. With one exception, (and even that, in its result, only proves the sanatory powers of the consolidation,) they have never jarred. Each has its sphere apart from the other—and each keeps in its sphere.

But the worst of such insidious articles as the *Sun's* is that they depress the idea of the sacredness of the *bond of union of these states.* That bond is the foundation of incomparably the highest political blessings enjoyed in the world! And the position of things at present demands that its sacredness should be recognized by *every and all* American citizens—however they may differ on points of doctrine or abstract rights.[36]

Whitman never modified his views concerning the sacredness and permanence of this bond. During the Civil War and afterwards, he expressed the belief that the main thing was and had been to "stick together." In such an instance, Whitman did not and would not concern himself with abstract rights or economic theories. According to Whitman's way of thinking, change and revolution might be permissible as long

[36] *Uncollected,* Vol. I, p. 156.

as there was no tampering with the bond of union. He subscribed whole-heartedly to Jackson's toast, "Our Federal union: it must be preserved!"

The Compromise dominated the political campaign of 1852. Both parties endorsed it but Winfield Scott, the Whig candidate who personally accepted the Compromise, was known to be the candidate of the Seward Whigs who did not. That the nation was tired of the slavery question was demonstrated by the election of Pierce even though there had been little enthusiasm for him. Pierce's administration was marked by more "manifest destiny," which resulted in the Gadsden purchase and an attempt to purchase Cuba. Internally, except for irritations arising out of the Fugitive Slave Law, the most significant bill was the Kansas-Nebraska Bill passed in 1854 which subdivided the Nebraska territory into two territories divided at Parallel 40, and provided that the territories could enter the Union either slave or free, dependent upon their respective constitutions. The slavery question was again opened, and civil war in Kansas was precipitated.

Stephen A. Douglas, of Illinois, chief architect of the bill, argued for squatter sovereignty, and later opposed the Dred Scott decision of 1857 which, while it decided that the Negro was not a citizen, also decided that the Missouri Compromise was unconstitutional. He also opposed the Lecompton Constitution which guaranteed the property in slaves that were already in Kansas and contained a special clause that would have denied the prospective state both the power to emancipate slaves without the consent of the owners and the power to forbid the entrance of slaves.[37]

Although Whitman was an anti-Lecomptonite, he was

[37] Faulkner, *op. cit.*, pp. 323-324.

pleased with the way things were progressing in Kansas. Though his knowledge of the matter was limited, he enthusiastically editorialized:

> Whether a pro-slavery constitution can be pushed down the stomachs of the people of Kansas, or whether it be submitted to the inhabitants of that territory for their fiat, the great cause of American White Work and Working People, will eventually gain, from either contingency. If the constitution be indeed formed upon the wishes of the people, no doubt or shadow of doubt clouds the prospects of the White race. But if slavery is put through under Buchanan, as it was under Pierce, the radical revolution in American politics will be sterner and more summary. The Black cause will enjoy a fleeting triumph in Kansas only to set in eternal darkness there—to be reprobated all over the North and West—and to be barred out indignantly from all fresh American States.[38]

The new constitution of Oregon was likewise hailed with joy. This editorial, written in 1858, stated in part:

> The new Constitution of Oregon prohibits colored persons, either slave or free, from entering the State—making an exclusively white population. This is objected to by several of the abolition Senators in the U.S. Senate—Mr. Hale and others. Mr. Seward, however is going to vote in favor of the Constitution.
>
> We shouldn't wonder if this sort of total prohibition of colored persons became quite a common thing in New Western, Northwestern, and even Southwestern States. If so, the whole matter of slavery agitation will assume another phase, different from any phase as yet. It will be a conflict between the totality of White Labor, on the one side, and on the other, the interference and

[38] *I Sit and Look Out*, p. 88.

competition of Black Labor, or of bringing in colored persons on any terms.

. . . .

So that prohibitions like that in the new Constitution of Oregon are not to be dismissed at first sight as arbitrary and unjust. We think the subject will bear much further examination. We even think it not unlikely but it would when examined meet the approval of the best friends of the Blacks, and the farthest-sighted opponents of Slavery. For, we repeat it, once get the slavery question to be argued on, as a question of White Workingmen's Labor against the Servile Labor of Blacks, and how many years would slavery stand in two-thirds of the present slave states?[39]

It is evident that Whitman's interest in slavery concerned itself chiefly with the effect that slavery had on the white workingmen. He declared the poor white man of the South to be absolutely worthless because he was unable to maintain a free economy in a section of the country dominated by a slave economy. Whitman did not recognize free Negro labor. Such interference and competition with white labor were not to be tolerated. How the free Negro was to make a living was of no concern to him. The country was large and growing larger, but it would never be large enough for both free white and free Negro labor. It is interesting to note that the Oregon editorial was written after two editions of *Leaves of Grass* (1855 and 1856) and after Whitman had proclaimed himself the poet of democracy.

However, Kansas rejected the Lecompton Constitution and did not join the Union until 1861, when she entered as a free state. The dispute had caused Free Soil democrats to demand that a new antislavery party

[39] *Ibid.*, pp. 89-90.

be formed on the principle of no further extension of slavery. The new Republican Party demanded the repeal of the Kansas-Nebraska Act and the Fugitive Slave Act and the abolition of slavery in the District of Columbia. At the same time, the anti-foreign, anti-Catholic Know Nothing Party was gaining in numbers. But the Know-Nothings split on the slavery issue. Democratic strength was declining in the North. The Republican Party was becoming a coalition party. Although Buchanan won the presidency in 1856, the Republicans made a good showing nationally.

Douglas broke with the Democratic Party over Kansas and began to recapture much of his popularity in the North, but many were troubled by his indifference to slavery. In 1858, he was opposed in his candidacy for re-election to the Senate from Illinois by Abraham Lincoln. The famous Lincoln-Douglas debates led to the "Freeport heresy" in which Douglas supported the Dred Scott decision in theory but insisted that in actuality slavery could exist only in a territory friendly to it. This doctrine lost Douglas the support of the South, split the Democratic Party, and prevented Douglas' election to the presidency in 1860.

John Brown's raid of 1859 stirred again the agitation against slavery and caused the South to demand further protective measures. Lincoln's election to the presidency in 1860 was looked upon by the South as a personal affront. The Republican Party had polled nearly all its votes in the free states so that Lincoln was a minority president. The Democratic Party had split when the Democratic Convention refused to accept a pro-slavery platform. After the election of Lincoln, South Carolina passed an ordinance of secession on December 20, 1860. Six other states had left the Union by February 4, 1861 and had organized the Confederate States of America. The stage was set for civil war.

But there were other aspects of the age equally as important as the economic and political issues. This was the age of the belief in the perfectibility of man and the equality of human rights. Great strides were made in social reform and in the attempt to emancipate the human spirit. One of the many reform movements took the form of Utopian communities. Robert Owen, an English manufacturer and philanthropist, visited the United States in 1824 and founded a community at New Harmony, Indiana. He believed that civilization had been constructed on the principle of individualism and selfishness, which were responsible for the evils men suffered. To eradicate these, the environment had to be perfected, for decent surroundings would make a good man. His community seemed on the verge of success, but Owen's radical views on religion and marriage brought discord and criticism.[40] The ideas of Charles Fourier were popularized in America by Albert Brisbane in his book, *The Social Destiny of Man*. Fourier wanted to organize mankind into groups or phalanxes of from three to eighteen hundred persons who would unite to carry on industry, art, and science. A large central building was to contain the workshop, the apartments for families, and the dining and meeting rooms. The buildings were to be surrounded by six thousand acres of farmland. Each man was to engage in the occupation he most enjoyed, but the least attractive work should be the best paid. Considerable freedom was to be allowed for personal taste and initiative. Fourier believed that in a large cooperative enterprise

[40] Harold Faulkner, *American Economic History* (New York, 1938), p. 370.

in which all worked for a common goal at the kind of labor each enjoyed, happiness would result. At least thirty-four phalanxes were organized in the various states before the movement failed. The best known phalanx was probably the Brook Farm experiment which included among its members such intellectuals of the period as George Ripley, Nathaniel Hawthorne, Charles A. Dana, and George Curtis. The experiment was watched with interest by other intellectuals including Ralph Waldo Emerson, A. Bronson Alcott, Horace Greeley, William H. Channing, Theodore Parker, and Margaret Fuller,[41] most of whom remained spectators.

The Icarian communities attempted to put into practice the communistic proposals of Etienne Cabet. The first settlement was made in Texas on the Red River in 1848. In 1849, the community moved to Nauvoo, Illinois. The Icarians met with indifferent success even though communities were established in Missouri, Iowa, and California.[42]

Whitman knew little about these schemes theoretically, and made little attempt to find out more. He wrote an editorial on the subject of Fourierism mainly to ridicule Horace Greeley, who had advocated several Utopian schemes in his New York *Tribune*. On the Brook Farm experiment, one that should have interested Whitman as a writer, there is no recorded comment. Whitman had no real interest in or sympathy for the Utopian communities of the day. He would have cared less for the various religious experiments such as the Harmony Society organized in 1805, the Separatists organized in 1817, and the Amana Society organized in 1859. Whitman would have objected to

[41] *Ibid.*, p. 372.
[42] *Ibid.*, p. 373.

many of the social and utopian schemes of the day because they were of foreign origin. It will be seen later that Whitman objected to America's following of foreign models and ideas.

During the same period attempts were made to revise the penal system. This was a movement with which Whitman was in complete sympathy. He was in favor of abolishing capital punishment although he had no objection to life imprisonment as a sentence for crimes then punishable by death. Several of the editorials in *I Sit and Look Out* are devoted to penal reform.

The Temperance Movement attracted Whitman's attention for a brief time, and besides various editorials on the subject, his novel, *Franklin Evans,* was a temperance tract. He also sympathized with the campaign for women's rights which was led by Lucretia Mott, Margaret Fuller, and Elizabeth Cady Stanton. He wrote editorials illustrating economic inequalities and the relationship between the low wages paid women workers and crime among women. His ideal woman, however, was the perfect wife and mother. But in none of the humanitarian fields can Whitman be called a crusader.

Labor in general was attempting to become articulate. The real labor movement began in 1827 when the Mechanics' Union of Trade Associations were organized. Ely Moore and John Ferrel were guiding fathers of the organization which claimed a membership of 300,000 and held annual conventions. The union disappeared in the panic of 1837. Between 1827 and 1837, the five national trade unions of cordwainers, comb makers, carpenters, hand-loom weavers, and printers were founded and pursued their purposes by means of political agitation as well as pressure on local employers. But workingmen's parties were never a success, and workingmen looked to the Loco-Foco wing of the Democratic Party for guidance. In 1840 President Van Buren gave impetus to labor reform by ordering the adoption of the ten-hour day on all government works. In 1842, the Massachusetts Supreme Court proclaimed the legality of labor unions, their purposes, and their methods.[43]

Whitman's ignorance of early trade unions and their activities seems strange when one considers that both Whitman and his father were carpenters and Whitman himself also a printer. Whitman, senior, died in 1855, and Whitman himself was carpentering between 1850 and 1855. Neither was a union member. Whitman had had, therefore, a definite connection with two of the earliest skilled groups to organize.

The issues emphasized by the early union leaders were hours of labor, wages, prices, paper money, public employment, factory legislation and the competition of women, prison competition, and freedom of the public lands. After, 1844, trade unionism often took the form of humanitarianism and socialistic efforts which resulted in experiments in communism and cooperation. One notable cooperative movement was the Granger Movement which began in 1867 and sought to eliminate some of the middleman's high charge by cooperative buying and selling, and to reduce railroad charges by obtaining legislation prescribing lower rates.[44] The Knights of Crispin, begun in 1869, were interested in the control of machinery. Occasional Fourieristic experiments were tried in various parts of the country,

[43] R. G. Gettell, *History of American Political Thought* (New York, 1928), p. 274.

[44] E. L. Bogart and D. L. Kemmerer, *Economic History of the American People* (New York, 1942), p. 508.

and once again labor attempted to make economic gains.

The Knights of Labor group was formed in Philadelphia by nine tailors in 1869. It was at first a secret organization with officers, ritual, and members all being known to the general public. The Knights believed that women should receive equal pay for equal work, that children under fourteen should be prohibited from working in shops, mines, and factories, that a work day should be eight hours, that wages should be paid once a week in money rather than in orders or scrip, that arbitration should be substituted for strikes, that public lands should be reserved for the actual settler, that cooperative institutions, productive and distributive, should be established, and that economic and social rights should be bestowed upon toilers in order that they might enjoy good government.[45] A series of successful strikes between 1884 and 1886 aided in the growth of the Knights of Labor into a powerful organization.

But the McCormick Reaper strike and the Haymarket Affair, although the Knights of Labor were not directly connected, marked a decline in the power of the organization. In 1885, it turned to politics and supported the campaign of Henry George.

Whitman never fought the battle of the free workingman and organized labor against hostile forces as he had fought the battle of the free white workingman against slave labor. He did sneer at manufacturers who cut wages and used the tariff as an excuse. He did advocate the payment of labor in hard money. He did advocate equal pay for women. He approved of short-

[45] Edward C. Kirkland, *A History of American Economic Life* (New York, 1932), p. 578.

ening the work day for clerks in stores, but he never campaigned for the rights of labor as he had campaigned for Free Soil. Whitman had a tendency to take the larger view whenever a practical problem came up for settlement. Free Soil could be treated as it affected the white workingman in mass. But the fate of a particular group of anthracite coal miners or the need for specific factory legislation was a more detailed problem. Traubel recorded Whitman as saying:

> I was in early life very bigoted in my anti-slavery, anti-capital-punishment and so on, but I have always had a latent toleration for the people who choose the reactionary course. The labor question was not up then as it is now—perhaps that's the reason I did not embrace it. It is getting to be a live question—someday will be the live question—then somebody will have to look out—especially the bodies with big fortunes wrung from the sweat and blood of the poor. This is all so— all of it so. Yet I do not feel as if I belonged to any one party.[46]

It is noticeable that the questions about which Whitman claimed to be bigoted in his views are subjects that he could treat exclusively, if he so desired, from a moral point of view. The solution of those problems could be postponed until the future. Whitman showed too, in this quotation, that he was not the perceiver but the accepter of conditions. If there had been agitation on the labor question, he would have had something to say. When there was agitation on the question, he had little meaningful to say. Certain economic conditions not readily attributable to slavery escaped his notice. Thus, Whitman attempted the over-all view of

[46] Horace Traubel, *With Walt Whitman in Camden,* Vol. I (New York, 1908), p. 193.

labor. He also believed that labor leaders had made a
mistake by not making their cause the cause of all men,
the over-all view. Still poverty and strikes could not be
completely ignored, not even by Whitman. Whitman
admitted that "the extreme poor suffer extra burdens
of life—carry an unfair load. Someday we will get that
fixed right in the world—someday after many days."[47]

The "someday after many days" would arrive for
Whitman when no man would be rich nor any man
poor, but all would be financially secure. In short, he
saw the alleviation of poverty not in the America of
today but in the world of tomorrow.

However the labor conflicts of 1877 and the poverty
and unemployment that prevailed caused Whitman to
fall back on a favorite device—the preparation of notes
for a lecture. These notes were published in *Specimen
Days and Collect* and justify strikes by noting that
the American Revolution and the French Revolution
were strikes against the monopoly of a few. Whitman
wrote:

> If the United States, like the countries of the Old
> World, are also to grow vast crops of poor, desperate,
> dissatisfied, nomadic, miserably-waged populations,
> such as we see looming upon us of late years—steadily,
> even if slowly, eating into them like a cancer of lungs
> or stomach—then our republican experiment, notwith-
> standing all its surface-successes, is at heart an un-
> healthy failure.

He concluded:

> Feb. '79.—I saw today a sight I had never seen be-
> fore—and it amazed, and made me serious; three quite
> good-looking American men, of respectable personal

[47] Traubel, *op. cit.*, Vol. II, p. 164.

appearance, two of them young, carrying chiffonier-bags on their shoulders, and the usual long iron hooks in their hands, plodding along, their eyes cast down, spying for scraps, bones, rags, &c.[48]

There is no doubt that the sight made Whitman serious, but most likely he thought of the day when poverty would be wiped from the face of the earth. Whitman admitted that he was not the type of man to take part in the scuffle. Consequently, he never squarely faced the present. Even his early writings were a blend of the present and the romantic. As he grew older, and looked upon himself as the poet of democracy, he was, of course, given to visionary conceptions. But for no major problem of his age can one go to Whitman for a proposed solution. He stated and discussed the problem, yes, but he left all solutions to time.

One particular work of Whitman's must be considered here. That work is a pamphlet or essay, "The Eighteenth Presidency," first published by Jean Catel and also included in Furness' *Walt Whitman's Workshop*. Proof sheets of this essay were found among Whitman's literary remains and indicate that evidently it was to have been published in 1856. Why it did not appear is something of a puzzle. That the essay was so incendiary no editor would publish it is not a sufficient reason. Whitman had already had a fling at being his own publisher and publicizer. Further in the essay, Whitman asked that others copy and distribute it. The essay is a call to the workingmen to throw off the stupidity of the three preceding presidencies, to repudiate any who jeopardized their free manhood. Whitman probably would have characterized the work as upbraiding, full of invective, and enthusiastic. Its keynote

[48] *Complete Prose*, p. 325.

is liberty. Although it offers no definite plan of action, it is political in subject matter. It is here that Whitman first expressed the idea that America had become too great for political parties and that one should vote for men rather than for parties.

This work represents one of Whitman's few attempts to act as a leader in the world of practical affairs, and it is possible that the work was never published because Whitman was unsure of his ability or his right to act as spokesman for the mass of workingmen on political issues. Since this essay was written ostensibly in support of the black Republicans, it is also possible that Whitman's break with the Democratic Party was not complete enough to allow him to publish the work, for even though Whitman later supported Lincoln in his campaign for a second term, he had looked to Douglas to organize a third party that would be completely neutral on the slavery question. Thus, a statement of Whitman's views that might have become definitive at a later date, remained unprinted until after his death.

Intellectually, the period from 1836 to 1860 was a stimulating one. The campaign for universal public education gained momentum, and though the ideal was not to be realized for several decades, public education made great strides. Reformers in the field emphasized the fact that democracy could survive only if the masses were educated. De Witt Clinton fought valiantly for the New York school system and Whitman supported that fight in his editorials in New York newspapers. Horace Mann succeeded in establishing normal schools for the training of teachers. Whitman was interested in teacher training and wrote in 1857:

There is a great truth underlying the Normal Schools. Every teacher, male and female, should be required

regularly to attend those schools all through their lives,
no matter how old they get to be..............

A grand Normal School in a city would be a fountain
of life for the entire education of that city. It should be,
in some respects, the noblest institution in the city.
It should keep up with the age, not fall behind it in any
respect. It should grade itself in science &c. by the
leading savants, the great reviews, the modern dis-
coveries and announcements. It should be the rendez-
vous of all mental authority.[49]

New colleges were established during the period until
by the end of 1860 there were 229 in the country.[50] The
Morrill Act of 1862 stimulated the establishment of
state universities. On the subject of education in general Whitman wrote:

The proper education of a child comprehends a great
deal more than is generally thought of. Sending him
to school and learning [sic] him to read and write, is
not educating him. That brings into play but a small
part of his power. A proper education unfolds and
develops every faculty in its just proportions. It com-
mences at the beginning, and leads him along the path
step by step. Its aim is not to give so much book-
learning, but to polish and invigorate the mind—to
make it used to thinking and acting for itself, and to
imbue it with a love for knowledge. It seeks to move
the youthful intellect to reason, reflect and judge, and
exercise its curiosity and powers of thought.[51]

And on the university level, Whitman believed:

The University while it forgets not to inculcate in
the scholar the necessity of attending to the material
agencies by which we are surrounded, is also occupied
with teaching him that there is something more than

[49] *I Sit and Look Out*, pp. 54-55.
[50] Gettell, *op. cit.*, p. 272.
[51] *Uncollected*, Vol. I, pp. 145-146.

matter in the universe, and instructs him in the art of
removing the integuments which cover the ideal, and
hide from all but the eye-intellectual the beauties and
truth of the immaterial world.[52]

Another great educational force was the lyceum. In
New England, there was hardly a village without a lyceum. The movement spread into the middle states and
some of the greatest intellects of the day gave their
best thought to the masses from the lecture platform.
Whitman heard Emerson and others lecture in New
York, but Whitman, himself, is not known to have been
a lyceum speaker. His fame as a writer came after the
lyceum movement had passed its peak.

Newspapers, too, stimulated intellectual growth. The
New York *Sun,* the first really successful penny newspaper, was established in 1833. Among America's greatest editors were the poet, William Cullen Bryant, who
became editor of the New York *Evening Post* in 1828,
and Horace Greeley, who founded the New York *Tribune* in 1841. Whitman, himself the editor of several New
York and Brooklyn newspapers, believed in the educational values of the newspaper. The penny press, he
wrote, carries "light and knowledge in among those
who most need it. They [the press] disperse the clouds
of ignorance, and make the great body of the people
intelligent, capable, and worthy of performing the
duties of republican freemen."[53]

The rising educational standards of the country made
possible the development of an American literature.
In 1837, Ralph Waldo Emerson delivered his Phi Beta
Kappa address, "The American Scholar," which has
been called the American intellectual declaration of

[52] *Ibid.,* p. 220.
[53] *Aurora,* pp. 111-112.

independence. The significant intellectual movement was transcendentalism, which grew out of Unitarianism. The tenets of this movement can be found in Emerson's little book *Nature*. Transcendentalism asserted the inalienable worth and divinity of man. It advocated the study and contemplation of nature. It believed that God and nature were contained in the mind. The high priest of transcendentalism was Emerson, whose essays Whitman read before 1855. Whitman acknowledged the influence of Emerson on his *Leaves of Grass* though he had at one time tried to deny that he had read Emerson until after the *Leaves* were first published. The letter written to Whitman by Emerson upon Whitman's publication of his *Leaves* in 1855 has been reproduced by nearly all of Whitman's biographers. Relationships between the two men were cordial although in his later years Whitman took a rather dim view of some of Emerson's works.

Another disciple of Emerson's, Thoreau, as well as the transcendentalist, A. Bronson Alcott, was known to Whitman and Whitman, though not an acknowledged member of the transcendental group, was influenced by the teachings of the group. Like all the transcendentalists, he believed the less government, the better. He wrote:

It needs that the machinery of government be simplified and narrowed—that a small circle be drawn, and that no stretching out thereof be permitted. Our republic is so extensive and contains such a variety of interests, that the legislature of the federal government is very apt to create clashings, and bickerings and jealousies. These are seen to increase year after year, and to become more and more dangerous to the stability of union. The only surety—the only real ground—the only certain shield—lies in letting each state manage its own affairs as unto it may seem best. And better still would it be to let smaller divisions, the local districts, the individual people, retain the rights and prerogatives of the *free man*, in their own respective hands.[54]

Further, Whitman had little respect for those who would blindly follow custom and the laws of the past. Legislatures of the past have been no different from those of the present. They were made up by men capable of making mistakes and subject to the various passions. Thus, the statute book is not to be revered because it is a product of the past. He wrote:

> We are free to confess, for ourself, that we have no reverence for the statute book, any further than it jibes with our notions of truth and justice. Government is at best but a necessary evil; and the less we have of it, the better.[55]

And again:

> We hesitate not to avow ourselves among the foremost of those who desire our experiment of man's capacity for self government, carried to its extreme verge. Every year, we wish to see the doors thrown wider, and the path made broader and broader. We delight in the progress of that doctrine which teaches to elevate the low and bring down the high.[56]

Unlike most of the other transcendentalists, he supported the Fugitive Slave Act. Though Whitman believed in the freedom of the individual, he thought first, always, of the Union and would preserve it at any cost.

The transcendentalists were Jeffersonian in their preference for the agrarian life. Nature was for them both a

[54] *Ibid.*, p. 91.
[55] *Ibid.*, p. 98.
[56] *Ibid.*, p. 90.

means of livelihood and a source of inspiration. Too many of the ills of society were attached to industrialization. Thoreau's retreat to Walden Pond and Hawthorne's participation in the Brook Farm experiment, although he was not a transcendentalist, showed the dissatisfaction of the transcendentalists with the industrial age in which they lived. Emerson criticized materialism, both black and white slavery, and the crassness of the age. A. Bronson Alcott experimented at his farm, Fruitlands, and later occupied himself with educational reforms. Thoreau denounced the world and withdrew to nature, which was the divine teacher and source of all inspiration.

Whitman was too much of a city man to be thoroughly agrarian. He felt that the mechanic and his occupation were the most important in America, and he gloried in every new technical advance. However, Whitman saw the country as a means of renewing man's vitality:

Democracy most of all affiliates with the open air, is sunny and hardy and sane only with Nature—just as much as Art is. Something is required to temper both— to check them, restrain them from excess, morbidity. I have wanted, before departure, to hear special testimony to a very old lesson and requisite. American Democracy, in its myriad personalities, in factories, work-shops, stores, offices—through the dense streets and houses of cities, and all their manifold sophisticated life—must either be fibred, vitalized, by regular contact with out-door light and air and growths, farm-scenes, animals, fields, trees, birds, sun-warmth and free skies, or it will certainly dwindle and pale. We cannot have grand races of mechanics, work people and commonalty, (the only specific purpose of America,) on any less terms. I conceive of no flourishing and heroic elements of Democracy maintaining itself at all, without the Nature-element forming a main part—to be its health-element and beauty-element—to really underlie the whole politics, sanity, religion and art of the New World.[57]

These ideas clearly relate to Whitman's concept of a spiritual democracy. Any attempt to relate them to agrarianism is defeated since one has no clear-cut idea as to whether spiritual renewal is to be gained through contemplation of the trees, birds, skies, fields, etc., or if one is to work in or among them.

In a more agrarian view, he wrote:

The final culmination of this vast and varied Republic will be the production and perennial establishment of millions of comfortable city homesteads and moderate-sized farms, healthy and independent, single separate ownership, fee simple, life in them complete but cheap, within reach of all. Exceptional wealth, splendor, countless manufactures, excess of exports, immense capital and capitalists, the five-dollar-a-day hotels well fill'd, artificial improvements, even books, colleges, and the suffrage—all, in many respects, in themselves, (hard as it is to say so, and sharp as a surgeon's lance,) form more or less, a sort of anti-democratic disease and monstrosity, except as they contribute by curious indirections to that culmination—seem to me mainly of value, or worth consideration, only with reference to it.

There is a subtle something in the common earth, crops, cattle, air, trees, &c., and in having to do at first hand with them, that forms the only purifying and perennial element for individuals and for society. I must confess I want to see the agricultural occupation of America at first hand permanently broaden'd. Its gains are the only ones on which God seems to smile. What others—what business, profit, wealth, without a

[57] *Complete Prose*, pp. 192-193.

taint? What fortune else—what dollar—does not stand for—and come from, more or less imposition, lying, unnaturalness?[58]

Even Whitman's views towards the West were not really agrarian but rather expansionist. He rhapsodized on the landscape and the men. He fell in love with the city of Denver. He hailed the rush into California in search of gold as a means of populating cities and towns in order that new states might soon enter the Union. His general attitude can be summed up in the following passage:

> Radical, true, far-scoped, and thorough-going Democracy may expect, (and such expecting will be realized,) great things from the West! The hardy denizens of those regions, where common wants and the cheapness of the land level conventionalism (that poison to the Democratic vitality,) begin at the roots of things—at first principles—and scorn the doctrines founded on mere precedent and imitation. . . . There is something refreshing even in the extremes, the faults, of Western character. Neither need the political or social fabric expect half as much harm from those untutored impulses, as from the staled and artificialized influence which enters too much into politics amid richer (not really richer, either) and older-settled sections.[59]

Although Whitman was not a true transcendentalist, there was much in his philosophy by a spiritual democracy that was traceable to transcendentalists. The ideas of the oneness of man, of man's identity with nature, and of the microcosm were all transcendental concepts. All the transcendental writers and Whitman were closer to the spirit of the age of the common man than

[58] *Ibid.*, pp. 332-333.
[59] *Uncollected*, Vol. I, p. 151.

the writers belonging to the so-called Brahmin group. This group included the historians, Prescott, Motley, and Parkman, and the poets Longfellow, Holmes, and Lowell. Prescott, Motley, and Parkman were romantic historians, and although Longfellow wrote some protest poetry, he is better known for his use of the romantic European and American past. Lowell is best represented by his literary criticism. The urbane wit of Holmes was in keeping with the genteel tradition. One Brahmin, George Bancroft, in his *History of the United States* was a militant democrat, but on the whole, the genteel writers were divorced from the age of the common man and from Whitman.

Two other writers who can not be assigned to either the transcendental group or the Brahmin group are Hawthorne and Melville. Both explored a facet of the American life and the American past. Both were concerned with sin or evil, a factor ignored by the transcendentalists and accepted but not interpreted by Whitman. Whitman's exact knowledge of these two men and their works cannot be ascertained, but he did know the works of both and wrote a brief review of Melville's *Mardi* which suggested that he had read or reviewed Melville's earlier romances *Typee* and *Omoo*.

Whitman's closest relations with a contemporary writer were, of course, with Emerson whom he acknowledged as his master, but his grasp of the intellectual movements of the day was of much the same calibre as his grasp of political and economic matters—general and not specific. Whitman was not a thorough student of contemporary ideas, intellectual, political, or social, for he strove for the over-all view.

Hence, an examination of Whitman's views in the light of his age, particularly during his formative years, shows him to be a mass of contradictions. Apparently Whitman often did not know what he believed on certain questions at any given time. He was a straw in the wind, and as the public showed interest in a question, Whitman expressed an opinion, most likely one in conformity with the views of the average man. His vacillation cannot be thoroughly accounted for by the statement that he matured late. The writings discussed were all composed after Whitman had loafed and invited his soul. Many were written after one and even two editions of *Leaves of Grass*. Whitman was not a true Jeffersonian, Jacksonian, or Abolitionist. One can say that he was a free trader and a free soiler. That his thinking was shallow is evident. His reading in economic theory was vague and indefinite, and no evidences of it are revealed in his writings. He was capable of invective and abuse, and often his appeal was made to the emotions rather than to reason. If America had attempted to follow the economic or political theories of Whitman, she would have foundered for want of a consistent plan.

Whitman trusted his instinct, primarily. That instinct was that of the average newspaper reader. The amazing thing about the various recollections of Whitman written by Carpenter, Johnston, Donaldson, and Kennedy is the dearth of ideas they reveal. The same thing holds true for Traubel's *With Walt Whitman in Camden*. Most of the chroniclers confine themselves to a description of the man's appearance and personality. Whitman's letters, too, are confined primarily to self. Take away from Whitman his declarations on the soundness of the mass of the people and there is little left in the way of ideas.

Yet Whitman's instincts were not sound enough to

save him from the expression of certain prejudices, some of which he never resolved. Over most of his prejudices, however, he was later able to throw a transcendental glow, and they are lost in the contemplation of his spiritual democracy. But justly to understand the limitations of Whitman's spiritual democracy and the place of the common man in this scheme, it is necessary to discover what Whitman actually thought of certain groups of people and his final conception of the common man. This material forms the subject matter of the next chapter.

CHAPTER II

Whitman's Attitude Toward Various Groups of People

WHITMAN EMPHASIZED the fact that his theme was democracy. Countless writers and biographers have followed his lead and examined his spiritual democracy. All assume that Whitman's poetry dealt with man in the abstract. Actually his theme was the liberty, fraternity, and equality which lead to the complete freedom, spiritual and political, of man. It was this aspect of Whitman's work which attracted the notice of European writers. Chapters like "Whitman in World Literature" in Frederick Schyberg's *Walt Whitman*,[1] and various studies showing Whitman's relationship to various European writers, usually propagandists for freedom, reveal to what extent Whitman's ideas of spiritual democracy fitted into the course of world-wide revolutionary literature. Yet Whitman cannot be thought of

[1] Among such studies are P. M. Jones, "Whitman, Verhaeren," Aberystwyth Studies, *University College Wales*, Vol. II (1914), pp. 71-106; H. F. Randall, "Whitman and Verhaeren—Priests of Human Brotherhood," *French Revue*, Vol. XVI (October, 1942), pp. 36-43; G. W. Allen, "Walt Whitman and Jules Michelet," *Etudes Anglaises*, Vol. I (May, 1937), pp. 230-37; Otto Springer, "Walt Whitman and Ferdinand Freiligrath," *American-German Review*, Vol. XI (December, 1944), pp. 22-26; Rea McCain, "Walt Whitman in Italy," *Italica*, Vol. XX (March, 1943), pp. 4-16; and Albert Parry, "Walt Whitman in Russia," *American Mercury*, Vol. XXXIII (September, 1934), pp. 100-107.

as the originator of a new outlook concerning man and his destiny. As Gay W. Allen wrote,

> The Whitmanesque thought was nothing new in 1855; it was an old story in Germany, France, and Scandinavia; it was "in the air"—and Whitman was a newspaper man at the time he was formulating his art and philosophy.[2]

Likewise, Esther Shephard in *Walt Whitman's Pose* has pointed out a source of inspiration and imitation in George Sand's *The Countess of Rudolstadt*. Although others had observed Whitman's debt to George Sand, Miss Shephard believed that Whitman took over the "character" of the carpenter-poet from Sand, and she has discovered numerous parallels between Whitman's poetic life and the Sand character. She summarized a phase of Whitman's life when she wrote:

> His pose as poet, derived from his identification of himself in America with George Sand's idealization of the greatest poet, was superimposed on the solid base of his phrenology and both combined to make his romanticized role as "wound-dresser" in the Civil War a natural one. Artful and egotistic as he was, he was able to make the duties that he took up pleasant and finally profitable, to himself and his reputation. He later made his work as government clerk fit into his "scheme" and his "theory" and in his old age in Camden, ministered to by his "housekeeper and friend," remaining blissfully ignorant of most of his household expenses and silencing any mention of them with a resounding "Ah" (and yet always, technically, financially independent), uttering his repeated swansongs, having modified naturally, if not logically, his early

[2] Gay W. Allen, "Walt Whitman—Nationalist or Proletarian?", *The English Journal*, Vol. XXVI (January, 1937), p. 52.

theory about the relation between health and art, still writing anonymous laudatory notices of himself and making provisions for what he termed his "future fame," forced to resort to lies, subterfuges, denials, mortally afraid, as it is said, in his last days, of the notebooks of his friends, he was able to keep up his pose to the last. Interestingly, we shall find that even his tomb belongs, in part at least, to his pose as George Sand's "poet." In his last anonymous descriptions of himself and in his last utterances and messages he is still the poet-at-large of humanity and the greatest lover.[3]

It is notable that Whitman never characterized any group of people in his own day as typically American. He did describe an occasional individual, primarily in hospital case-histories, as a typical American, but the general class of Americans escaped him. Professor Allen admitted that "perhaps no poet ever understood the average American less than Whitman did. In fact he would probably have remained forever a literary failure had not some English intellectuals discovered and press-agented him."[4]

It would not be too far wrong to say that Whitman misunderstood the role America was to play in the world to come. If America was to be a haven for the oppressed and a refuge for immigrants from all over the world, it was inevitable that her culture would be shaped from without as well as from within. It was also inevitable that various immigrant groups would be slow to assimilate the American idea and ideal, provided that that idea and ideal were utterly foreign to their previous ways of thinking and living, and that such groups would be exploited both politically and economically

[3] Esther Shephard, *Walt Whitman's Pose* (New York, 1936), pp. 263-264.

[4] Allen, *op. cit.*, p. 49.

by certain groups of Americans. An impatience with America as she actually was, an impatience with and a dislike for specific groups of people, is evident throughout Whitman's life and works. Although he directed his song to the American common man first, and then to the common man of the world, Whitman's American common man, in daily living, did not include all who dwelled within the territorial borders of the United States. Emory Holloway attempted to resolve some of these inconsistencies in Whitman's early thought. "His faith in the 'average man' had as yet no universal application. It applied only to America, the America he knew, where the average man was an Anglo-Saxon freeholder dwelling in the holy land of democracy."[5]

Whitman made much of his English-Dutch ancestry, dwelling particularly on the Dutch strain. His autobiographical notes, which he gave to Bucke for his Whitman biography, emphasized what might be called his Anglo-Saxon heritage. A reason for Whitman's continued toleration for the South and the actions of the South might be found in the fact that before the Civil War, the white South had received few immigrants and, exclusive of Louisiana and the Gulf regions, was predominantly Anglo-Saxon. Whitman even went so far as to see the winning of battles in the Mexican War as another proof of the indomitable energy of the Anglo-Saxon character. Obviously, the groups of people that Whitman would welcome to the country would be those with Anglo-Saxon characteristics.

Whitman also had definite views to express concerning the fate of the original settlers of America, the Indians. In *Brooklyniana,* the Indian came in for his

[5] Emory Holloway, *Whitman, An Interpretation in Narrative* (New York, 1926), p. 30.

share of romanticizing and Whitman clung to Indian place names. In *An American Primer*, an assortment of Whitman lecture notes on language which Traubel printed, Whitman wrote:

> What name a city has—What name a State, river, sea, mountain, wood, prairie, has,—is not indifferent matter.—All aboriginal names sound good. I was asking for something savage and luxuriant, and behold here are the aboriginal names. I see how they are being preserved. They are honest words—they give the true length, breadth, depth. They fit. Mississippi—the word winds with chutes—it rolls a stream three thousand miles long. Ohio, Connecticut, Ottawa, Monongahela, all *fit*.[6]

Hence, the Indian and his place names were to supply the background for native America which was to be developed by the invading white man. Along these same lines, Traubel recorded Whitman as saying:

> I think now is the time for archaeology to be exploited here anyhow—especially American archaeology. I remember that when Lord Houghton, Moncton Milnes called to see me years ago, the first thing he said to me was: "Your people don't think enough of themselves: are not in the good sense patriotic enough: they do not realize that they not only have a present but a past, the traces of which are rapidly slipping away from them." He referred to the slack interest we show in "remains." We have our schools and expeditions for Greek exploration: the people concerned are begging, begging, all the time for money—which is all right, as far as it goes. I would not put a straw in the way of this—not a straw: I wish it well: it is important work.

[6] Horace Traubel, ed., *An American Primer by Walt Whitman* (Boston, 1904), pp. 17-18.

But I say, why not open up our own past—exploit the American contribution to this important science.[7]

Whitman was well aware that the only past of archaeological interest that America possesses was the Indian past. Whitman had completely taken over this past as a part of the American heritage, but he did not accept the Indian along with his past even though he could write of him in this fashion in "An Indian Bureau Reminiscence":

There is something about the aboriginal Americans, in their highest characteristic representations, essential traits, and the ensemble of their physiques and physiognomy—something very remote, very lofty, arousing comparisons with our own civilized ideals—something that our literature, portrait painting, &c., have never caught and that will almost certainly never be transmitted to the future, even as a reminiscence. No biographer, no historian, no artist, has grasped it—perhaps could not grasp it. It is so different, so far outside our standards of eminent humanity. Their feathers, paint—even the empty buffalo skull—did not, to say the least, seem any more ludicrous to me than many of the fashions I have seen in civilized society. I should not apply the word savage (at any rate, in the usual sense) as a leading word in the description of those great aboriginal specimens, of whom I certainly saw many of the best. There were moments, as I looked at them or studied them, when our own exemplification of personality, dignity, heroic presentation anyhow (as in the conventions of society, or even in the accepted poems and plays,) seemed sickly, puny, inferior.[8]

[7] Horace Traubel, *With Walt Whitman in Camden*, Vol. I (New York, 1908), pp. 128-129.

[8] *Complete Prose*, pp. 412-413.

Although the preceding quotation is laudatory, the Indian is treated as a man with a past, not as a man with a present and a future. Although Whitman proclaimed that America was for everybody, he felt that the Indian, as well as the Negro, would be eliminated. Traubel recorded Whitman as saying:

> ". . . . it is the law of races, history, what-not; always so far inexorable—always to be. Someone proves that a superior grade of rats comes and then all the minor rats are cleared out." I said: "That sounds like Darwin." "Does it? It sounds like me, too."[9]

Whitman did not believe in the amalgamation of the races, and the Indians were not to be allowed to exist as an independent race of people. It cannot be doubted that if Whitman had been old enough to write editorially at the time of Jackson's ignoring of the rights of the Indian nations of Georgia, he would have sanctioned Jackson's disregard of the rights granted the Indians through treaties, but he would have justified his stand by asserting the impossibility of allowing any individual nation to exist within the territorial bounds of the United States.

The Indians in Canada did not escape Whitman's notice, and in his diary and account of his Canadian visit he wrote:

> Went down to an Indian settlement at Ah-me-ja-wah-noong (i. e. the Rapids) to visit the Indians, the Chippewas. Not much to see of novelty—in fact, nothing at all of aboriginal life or personality; but I had a fine drive with the gentleman that took me—Dr. McLane, the physician appointed by the government for the

[9] Traubel, *With Walt Whitman in Camden*, Vol. II, p. 283. Whitman used the word "eliminated" when he spoke of the fate of the Indian and the Negro in America.

tribe. There is a long stretch, three or four miles, front-
ing the St. Clair, south of Sarnia, running back, easterly
nearly the same distance, good lands for farming and
rare sites for building—and this is the "reservation" set
apart for these Chips. There are said to be four hundred of them, but I could not see evidences of one
quarter of that number. There are three or four neat
third-class wooden dwellings, a church, and council-
house, but the less said about the rest of the edifices the
better. "Every prospect pleases," as far as land, shore,
and water are concerned, however. The Dominican
government keeps entire faith with these people (and
all its Indians, I hear), preserves these reservations to
live on, pays them regular annuities, and whenever any
of their land is sold, puts the proceeds strictly in their
funds. Here they farm languidly (I saw some good
wheat), fish, etc.; but the young men generally go off
to hire as laborers and deck-hands on the water. I saw
and conversed with Wa-wa-nosh, the interpreter, son
of a former chief. He talks and writes as well as I do.
In a nice cottage near by lived his mother, who doesn't
speak anything but Chippewa. There are no very old
people. I saw one man of thirty in the last stages of
consumption. This beautiful and ample tract, in its
present undeveloped condition, is quite an eyesore to
the Sarnians.[10]

Thus, one can see Whitman's displeasure with the
Indians in Canada. On their beautiful and ample
reservation, under the watchful eye of a strictly fair
government, they had done nothing to improve their
lot. Even the signs of aboriginal life had disappeared.
These Canadian Indians did little to dispel Whitman's
general view toward all Indians that

[10] W. S. Kennedy, *Walt Whitman's Diary in Canada* (Boston, 1904),
pp. 9-10.

. . . the several specimens of men, women, and children whom I saw were quite enough to take poetry out of one's aboriginal ideas. They are degraded, shiftless and intemperate—very much after the lowest class of blacks. They glean a sort of living out of their free range of the peninsula before mentioned, and by working for the farmers in harvest time, and selling baskets, mats, and wooden ware, in making which they are very handy. The best thing connected with these poor devils is that they are not very thievish—perhaps considering their poverty, less so than any known race of people.[11]

Even in *Leaves of Grass*, the Indian was marked as the man who must vanish. Whitman loved the Indian for the past with which he had to become a representative of Whitman's native American man. The sound and majesty of Indian names and the fate of the Indian are celebrated in the lines:

On my way a moment I pause
Here for you! and here for America!
Still the present I raise aloft, still the future of the
    States I harbinger glad and sublime,
And for the past I pronounce what the aid holds of the
    red aborigines.

The red aborigines,
Leaving natural breaths, sounds of rain and winds, calls
    as of birds and animals in the woods, syllabled to us
    for names,
Okonee, Koosa, Ottawa, Monongahela, Sauk, Natchez,
    Chattahoochee, Kaqueta, Oronoco,
Wabash, Miami, Saginaw, Chippewa, Oshkosh, Walla-
    Walla,

[11] *Uncollected,* Vol. I, p. 317.

Leaving such to the States they melt, they depart,
    charging the water and land with names.[12]

Thus, the Indian is a man with a past but no present
or future. The following Whitman sketches are illustrative:

In arriere the peace-talk with the Iroquois, the aborig-
    ines, the calumet, the pipe of good-will, arbitration
    and indorsement,
The sachem blowing the smoke first toward the sun and
    then toward the earth,
The drama of the scalp-dance enacted with painted
    faces and guttural exclamations,
The setting out of the war-party, the long and stealthy
    march, slaughter of enemies;[13]

and

When his hour for death had come,
He slowly rais'd himself from the bed on the floor,
Drew on his war-dress, shirt, leggings, and girdled the
    belt around his waist,
Call'd for vermilion paint (his looking glass was held
    before him,)
Painted half his face and neck, his wrists, and back-
    hands,
Put the scalp-knife carefully in his belt—then lying
    down resting a moment,
Rose again, half sitting, smiled, gave in silence his
    extended hand to each and all,
Sank faintly low to the floor (tightly grasping the toma-
    hawk handle,)

[12] Walt Whitman, "Starting from Paumanok," *Complete Writings
of Walt Whitman* edited by Bucke, Harned, and Traubel (New
York, 1902), Vol. VIII, p. 30. Hereafter referred to as *Complete
Writings*.
[13] "Our Old Feuillage," *Complete Writings*, Vol. X, p. 19.

Fix'd his look on wife and little children—the last:
(And here a line in memory of his name and death.)[14]

A picture of an Indian woman of the present is given
in "The Sleepers":

A red squaw came one breakfast-time to the old home-
   stead,
On her back she carried a bundle of rushes for rush-
   bottoming chairs,
Her hair, straight, shiny, coarse, black, profuse, half-
   envelop'd her face,
Her step was free and elastic, and her voice sounded
   exquisitely as she spoke.

My mother look'd in delight and amazement at the
   stranger,
She look'd at the freshness of her tall-borne face and
   full and pliant limbs,
The more she look'd upon her she loved her,
Never before had she seen such wonderful beauty and
   purity,
She made her sit on a bench by the jamb of the fireplace,
   she cook'd food for her,
She had no work to give her, but she gave her remem-
   brances and fondness.[15]

Of course, this sketch celebrated Whitman's mother
as well as the Indian woman, but it does serve to
illustrate that the Indian and his occupation are not a
part of

The main shapes [that] arise!
Shapes of Democracy total, result of centuries,
Shapes ever projecting other shapes,
Shapes of turbulent many cities,

[14] "Osceola," *Complete Writings*, Vol. X, p. 19.
[15] *Complete Writings*, Vol. IX, p. 207.

Shapes of the friends and home-givers of the earth,
Shapes bracing the earth and braced with the whole
   earth.[16]

Probably Whitman's final views on the destiny of the
Indians are summed up in the poem "Yonnondia."

A Song, a poem of itself—the word itself a dirge,
Amid the wilds, the rocks, the storm and wintry night,
To me such misty, strange tableaux the syllables calling
   up;
Yonnondia—I see, far in the west or north, a limitless
   ravine, with plains and mountains dark,
I see swarms of stalwart chieftains, medicine-men, and
   warriors,
As flitting by like clouds of ghosts, they pass and are
   gone in the twilight.
(Race of the woods, the landscapes free, and the falls!
No picture, poem, statement, passing them to the
   future.)
Yonnondia! Yonnondia!—unlimn'd they disappear;
Today gives place, and fades—the cities, farms, factories
   fade;
A muffled sonorous sound, a wailing word is borne
   through the air for a moment,
Then blank and gone and still, and utterly lost.[17]

Such are Whitman's views on the Indian. That the
Indian was disappearing was regrettable but right, for
it was a circumstance that could not be prevented. The
Indian was to be allowed no place in the developing
society, and his contribution could only be the
bequeathal of his past to the conquerors of his land.
Whitman did not feel that the Indian had been misused.
To him, the Indians who yet remained had misused the

[16] "Song of the Broad-Axe," *Complete Writings*, Vol. VIII, p. 237.
[17] *Complete Writings*, Vol. IX, p. 310.

privileges granted them by a benevolent government. One need only refer to the sketch of the Canadian Indians to discover this facet of Whitman's thought. Whitman generally excluded the Indian from his catalogues because he could find no place for the only truly native American man. Hence, there is no contradiction in either Whitman's poetry or prose concerning his final conception of the destiny of the Indian.

Since Whitman believed that the Indian would be and should be eliminated, his views on another of the darker races of people, the Negro, are provocative. Whitman's equivocal views on slavery and his dislike for abolitionists have been mentioned by numerous biographers who ascribe the break between William O'Connor and Whitman to the former's over-zealous abolitionism. Whitman's position had been justified by some of his followers on the premise that his belief in an idealistic spiritual democracy recognized the equality and divinity of the soul of man, and hence Whitman believed the institution of slavery to be evil since it denied this equality. Such an idea is expressed in these lines from a rejected poem:

> I say man shall not hold property in man;
> I say the least developed person on earth is just as important and sacred to himself or herself, as the most developed person is to himself or herself.

> I say where liberty draws not the blood out of slavery, there slavery draws the blood out of liberty,
> I say the word of the good old cause in These States, and resound it hence over the world.[18]

But on a more realistic level, Whitman's views can be summed up as follows:

[18] "Says," *Complete Writings*, Vol. X, p. 301.

Of the Negro, as a race he had a poor opinion. He said that there was in the constitution of the negro's mind an irredeemable trifling or volatile element and that he would never amount to much in the scale of civilization. I never knew him to have a friend among the negroes while he was in Washington, and he never seemed to care for them, or they for him, although he never manifested any particular aversion to them. In defence of the negro's capabilities I once cited to him Wendell Phillips' eloquent portrait of Toussaint L'Ouverture, the pure black Haytian warrior and statesman. . . . He thought it a fancy picture much overdrawn, and added humorously, paraphrasing Betsy Prig in 'Martin Chuzzlewit,' 'I don't believe there was no such nigger.'[19]

"I don't believe there was no such nigger" was probably Whitman's answer to the letter written by Elisa Seaman Leggett describing Sojourner Truth and her activities.[20] He certainly would not have been impressed by Sojourner's identifying her utterances as from God and denying the necessity of knowing the writer's name for she considered all great utterances as coming from God. Rather, Whitman would have seen no reason to change his opinion expressed in 1858:

Who believes that the Whites and Blacks can ever amalgamate in America? Or who wishes it to happen? Nature has set an impassable seal against it. Besides, is not America for the Whites? And is it not better so? As long as the Blacks remain here how can they become anything like an independent and heroic race? There is no chance for it.

Yet we believe there is enough material in the colored

[19] Clara Barrus, *Whitman and Burroughs, Comrades* (New York, 1931), p. 335.
[20] Thomas Donaldson, *Walt Whitman, the Man* (New York, 1896), pp. 243-46.

race, if they were in some secure and ample part of the earth, where they would have a chance to develope [sic] themselves, to gradually form a race, a nation that would take no mean rank among the people of the world. They would have the good will of all the civilized powers, and they would be compelled to look upon themselves as freemen, capable, self-reliant—mighty. Of course all this, or anything toward it, can never be attained by the Blacks here in America.[21]

That the Negro had spent two and a half centuries in involuntary servitude in this country meant little to Whitman. That the Negro had made the prosperity of a certain section of the country meant less except where the forced labor of the Negro infringed upon the rights of free white workingmen. But the free Negro was not to be tolerated either. He was to be dismissed from America for America was to be a land for white men only. Even during the Civil War, Whitman found it hard to accept the Negroes in the Union Army. He seemingly kept looking for these troops to make major blunders. In *November Boughs,* Whitman wrote:

One of my war time reminiscences comprises the quiet side scene of a visit I made to the First Regiment U. S. Color'd Troops, at their encampment, and on the occasion of their first paying off, July 11, 1863. Though there is now no difference of opinion worth mentioning, there was a powerful opposition to enlisting blacks during the earlier years of the secession war. Even then, however, they had their champions. "That the color'd race," said a good authority, "is capable of military training and efficiency, is demonstrated by the eagerness displayed in raising, organizing, and drilling of African troops. Few white regiments make a better appearance on parade than the First and Second Loui-

[21] *I Sit and Look Out,* p. 90.

siana Native Guards. The same remark is true of other
color'd regiments. At Milliken's Bend, at Vicksburg, at
Port Anderson, on Morris Island, and wherever tested,
they have exhibited determin'd bravery, and com-
pell'd the plaudits alike of the thoughtful and thought-
less soldiery. During the siege of Fort Anderson the
question was often ask'd those who beheld their resolute
charges, how the 'niggers' behav'd under fire; and without exception the answer was complimentary to them.
'O tip-top!' 'first-rate!' 'bully!' were the usual replies."
But I did not start out to argue the case—only to give
my reminiscence literally, as jotted on the spot at the
time.[22]

Note that the preceding is a quotation within a quotation. This enclosed quotation does not necessarily state
the Whitman view for he did consider the matter
a question for argument and implied such in the last
sentence. Whitman seemed to be trying to convince
himself of the worth of the Negro soldiery. A truer concept of Whitman's beliefs as to the value and worth of
the Negro soldiery can be gained from the following
letter written by him to the editor of the Brooklyn *Eagle*
in 1864:

The public mind is deeply excited and righteously so,
at the starvation of the United States prisoners of war in
the hands of the Secessionists. The dogged sullenness
and scoundrelism prevailing everywhere among the
guards and officials, (with, I think the general exception
of the surgeons,) the measureless torments of the forty
or fifty thousand helpless young men, with all their
humiliation, hunger, cold, filth, despair, hope utterly
given out, and the more and more frequent imbecility,
I have myself seen the proofs of in so many instances,
that I know the facts well, and know that the half has

[22] *Complete Prose*, pp. 420-421.

not been told, nor tithe either. But there is another and full as important side to the story. Whose fault is it at bottom, that our men have not been exchanged? To my knowledge it is understood by Col. Mulford, our capital Executive Officer of Exchange, and also by those among us who have had longest and nearest contact with the secession exchange officers, that the Government of the latter have been and are ready to exchange man for man as far as prisoners go, (certainly all the whites, and, as I understand it, a large proportion of the blacks also).

Under the President (whose humane, conscientious and fatherly heart, I have abiding faith in,) the control of exchange has remained with the Secretary of War, and also with such persons as Major General Butler and Major General Hitchcock. In my opinion the Secretary has taken and obstinately held a position of cold-blooded policy, (that is he thinks it policy,) more cruel than anything done by the Secessionists. Ostensibly and officially saying he will not exchange at all, unless the Secession leaders will give us, on average terms, all the blacks they capture in military action; the Secretary has also said (and this is the basis of his course and policy,) that it is not for the benefit of the Government of the United States that the power of the Secessionists should be repleted by some 50,000 men in good condition now in our hands, besides getting relieved of the support of nearly the same number of human wrecks and ruins, of no advantage to us, now in theirs.

Major General Butler, in my opinion, has also incorporated in the question of exchange a needless amount of personal pique, and an unbecoming obstinacy. He, too, has taken his stand on the exchange of all black soldiers, has persisted in it without regard to consequences, and has made the whole of the large and complicated question of general exchange turn upon that one item alone, while it is but a drop in the bucket.

Then he makes it too much a personal contest who shall conquer, and an occasion to revenge the bad temper and insults of the South toward himself.

Of Major General Hitchcock, the public may judge what a valuable contribution he brings to this matter of exchange, from a remark he has made not long since, that "none but cowards are ever taken prisoners in war."

This is the spirit in which the faith of the Government of the United States toward fifty thousand of its bravest young men—soldiers faithful to it in its hours of extremest peril—has been, for the past year, and is now handled. Meantime, while the thing has been held in abeyance in this manner, considerably more than one-fourth of those helpless and most wretched men, (their last hours passed in the thought that they were abandoned by their Government, and left to their fate,) have been exchanged by deaths of starvation, (Mr. Editor, or you, reader, do you know what a death by starvation actually is?) leaving half the remainder closely prepared to follow, from mental and physical atrophy; and even the remnant cannot long tarry behind. So that the Secretary and the Major-Generals mentioned may find their policy work out even more than they calculated.

In my opinion, the anguish and death of these ten to fifteen thousand American young men, with all the added and incalculable sorrow, long drawn out, amid families at home, rests mainly upon the heads of members of our own government; and if they persist, the death of the remainder of the Union prisoners and often worse than death, will be added.[23]

The attitude of Walt Whitman here demonstrated is that attitude which would sacrifice any number of

[23] Quoted in Charles I. Glicksberg, *Walt Whitman and the Civil War* (Philadelphia, 1933), pp. 178-180.

Negro soldiers in Secessionist hands in order to redeem one white soldier. If Whitman knew as much about Southern prison camps as he claimed, he knew also that the fate of the Negro prisoners was much more severe than that of white soldiers, severe though that was. It is probable that the Secretary of War and the commanding generals felt that the Negro soldiers who had served the Union Army loyally and well should not be deserted. Whitman did not share this feeling. It was obviously his opinion that the question of exchanging Negro soldiers was of no importance—a mere drop in the bucket—whereas the exchanging of white soldiers was of paramount importance. Thus, Whitman could not even bring himself to look upon prisoners of war in the same manner but sentimentally appealed for the relief of white prisoners even though that relief might be gained through the further suffering of Negro prisoners.

Another view of Whitman's attitude towards the Negro soldiery is seen in his account of the paying off of the First U. S. Colored Troops:

> Now the paying is to begin. The Major (paymaster) with his clerk seat themselves at a table—the rolls are before them—the money box is open'd—there are packages of five, ten, twenty-five cent pieces. Here comes the first Company (b), some 82 men, all blacks. Certes, we cannot find fault with the appearance of this crowd —negroes though they be. They are many enough, bright enough, look as if they had the soldier-stuff in them, look hardy, patient, many of them real handsome young fellows. The paying, I say, has begun. The men are march'd up in close proximity. The clerk calls off name after name, and each walks up, receives his money, and passes along out of the way. It is a real

study, both to see them come close, and to see them
pass away, stand counting their cash—(nearly all of this
company get ten dollars and three cents each). The
clerk calls George Washington. That distinguish'd per-
sonage steps from the ranks, in the shape of a very
black man, good sized and shaped, and aged about 30,
with a military mustache; he takes his "ten three," and
goes off evidently well pleas'd. (There are about a
dozen Washingtons in the Company. Let us hope that
they do honor to the name.) At the table, how quickly
the Major handles the bills, counts without trouble,
everything going on smoothly and quickly. The regiment numbers today about 1,000 men (including 20
officers, the only whites).

Now another company. These get $5.36 each. The
men look well. They, too, have great names; besides the
Washingtons aforesaid, John Quincy Adams, Daniel
Webster, Calhoun, James Madison, Alfred Tennyson,
John Brown, Benj. G. Tucker, Horace Greeley, &c. The
men step off aside, count their money with a pleas'd
half-puzzl'd look. Occasionally, but not often, there are
some thoroughly African physiognomies, very black in
color, large protruding lips, low forehead, &c. But I
have to say that I do not see one utterly revolting face.[24]

The group of Negroes here discussed intrigued Whitman; yet, they did little to allay his doubts concerning
Negroes as a whole. Though these men might be hardy,
alert, and intelligent, they could not typify for Whitman, characteristic American virtues. On one occasion,
Whitman had objected to the use of the Negro to demonstrate features of Americanism even in art.[25] Thus, it
is significant that the Negro soldier is mentioned but

[24] *Complete Prose*, pp. 421-422.
[25] While visiting an art exhibit, Whitman preferred a picture of a
boy with a flute, painted by William Sidney Mount, to Mount's picture
with a Negro as the subject, since "Mount's negro may be said to
have a character of Americanism, too; but I must be pardoned for

briefly in *Specimen Days* and not at all in *Drum-Taps*.
Rather, the Negro appeared only in the poem "Ethiopia
Saluting the Colors" and here is a female peasant:

Who are you dusky woman, so ancient hardly human,
With your wooly-white and turban'd head, and bare
    bony feet?
Why, rising by the roadside here, do you the colors
    greet?

('Tis while our army lines Carolina's sands and pines,
Forth from thy hovel door thou Ethiopia com'st to me;
As under doughty Sherman I march toward the sea.)

*Me master years a hundred since from my parents
    sunder'd*
*A little child, they caught me as the savage beast is
    caught,*
Then hither me across the sea the cruel slaver brought.

No further does she say, but lingering all the day,
Her high-borne turbanned head she wags, and rolls her
    darkling eye,
And courtesies to the regiments, the guidons moving
    by.

What is it fateful woman, so blear, hardly human?
Why wag your head with turban bound, yellow, red
    and green?
Are the things so strange and marvelous you see or
    have seen?[26]

---

saying, that I never will admire the exemplifying of our national attributes with Ethiopian minstrelsy, or Yankee Hill Characters upon the
state, as the best and highest we can offer in that way." *Uncollected*,
Vol. I, p. 238. Mount cannot be characterized as a painter of Negro
minstrelsy for his scenes usually depicted rural scenes of Negroes and
whites at work or play as well as drawing room scenes.

[26] *Complete Writings*, Vol. IX, pp. 84-85.

The heroic deeds, the silent suffering, the magnificent courage of the soldiers both Northern and Southern might include the Negro generally, but he specifically ignored the Negro in his summing up and extolling of the virtues of the American male during the war.

After the war, Whitman felt that the Negro was unfit for freedom. A group of Washington Negroes, celebrating the election of an official interested in their welfare, filled him with loathing. Whitman expected, unjustly, that the newly freed Negroes would be immune to political exploitation and intimidation. After having been denied all rights and privileges and even having been prevented in most instances from learning to read and to write, he expected the Negroes to belie his own belief that they were ignorant. The celebrated estrangement between William O'Connor and Whitman originated in an argument over the Fifteenth Amendment to the Constitution:

> O'Connor became enraged at what Walt said about the unfitness of the negroes for voting. They were in the habit of goring each other in argument like two bulls, and that time Walt was, I guess, rather brutal and insulting. It was in O'Connor's home. O'Connor fired up and turned on him. Walt took his hat and went home in a pet. Then when they met on the street the next day, Walt put out his hand; but William shied around and went on past. The iron had entered his soul.[27]

Later, Traubel records Whitman as discussing the Negro as follows:

> Traubel said: "The Republicans make a good deal of the negro vote—the suppressed vote." "So they do," said W., "and that they have a right to do: I, too, em-

[27] Barrus. *op. cit.*, p. 98.

phasize that: it's a point not to be dodged or trifled with: but after every allowance is made the fact still remains true: the white people of a number of States are nearly unanimous in their antagonism.[28]

Notwithstanding the generalizations on equality uttered by the poet of democracy, the white people of a number of states were kindred souls to Walt Whitman in their antagonism toward the Negro's power to vote. One finds no statement of Whitman's objecting to grandfather clauses and other devices, legal and extralegal, aimed at depriving the Negro of his right to vote. Rather, Whitman's view can be found in this note of 1874:

> As if we had not strained the voting and digestive calibre of American Democracy to the utmost for the last fifty years with the millions of ignorant foreigners, we have now infused a powerful percentage of blacks, with about as much intellect and calibre (in the mass) as so many baboons. But we stood the former trial—solved it—and though this is much harder, will I doubt not, triumphantly solve this.[29]

Feeling as he did about the general capabilities of the Negro, it is not surprising that in answering Carlyle's "Shooting Niagara," Whitman let Carlyle have his say on the subject of Negro emancipation without reply.[30] Whitman could feel that the Negro question was a problem but that the Negro would get his due from the Negro, a rather cryptic utterance, and could conclude:

[28] Traubel, Vol. III, p. 69.
[29] *Uncollected*, Vol. II, p. 57.
[30] See Gregory Paine, "Literary Relations of Whitman and Carlyle with Especial Reference to their Contrasting Views on Democracy," *Studies in Philology*, Vol. XXXVI (1939), pp. 550-563.

The American white and the Southern black will *mix* but not *ally*. I have considered the problem from all sides. It is wonderful the readiness with which French and Negro, or Spanish and Negro will marry—interlock—and the results are always good. It is the same with the Injun and Nigger—they too will ask no questions: they, too, achieve equally fine reproductivities. . . . Now the Southern white does not encourage such intermixtures: there are psychological, physiological, reasons for it—back of all psychologies, physiologies, some deeper fact.[31]

Note that the white is characterized as both American and Southern, but Whitman did not refer to the American Negro in his writings, for the Negro, as well as the Indian, would vanish since the Negro could not compete with the white. Since all that America had to do was to wait for the gradual extinction of the darker races of people, Whitman might be construed as advocating genocide in the United States.

The free Negro in America does not find a place in *Leaves of Grass*. There are several famous pictures of the slave Negro, one of them being the picturesque,

> The negro holds firmly the reins of his four horses, the block swags underneath on its tied-over chain,
> The negro that drives the long dray of the stone-yard, steady and tall he stands pois'd on one leg on the string-piece,
> His blue shirt exposes his ample neck and breast and loosens over his hip-band,
> His glance is calm and commanding, he tosses the slouch of his hat away from his forehead,
> The sun falls on his crispy hair and mustache, falls on the black of his polish'd and perfect limbs.[32]

[31] Traubel, Vol. II, p. 283.
[32] *Complete Writings*, Vol. VIII, p. 46.

Whitman's view of the spiritual brotherhood of man is exemplified in the lines:

> The runaway slave came to my house and stopt outside,
> I heard his motions crackling the twigs of the woodpile,
> Through the swung half-door of the kitchen I saw him limpsy and weak,
> And went where he sat on a log and led him in and assured him,
> And brought water and fill'd a tub for his sweated body and bruis'd feet,
> And gave him a room that enter'd from my own, and gave him some coarse clean clothes,
> And remember perfectly well his revolving eyes and his awkwardness,
> And remember putting plasters on the galls of his neck and his ankles;
> He staid with me a week before he was recuperated and pass'd north,
> I had him sit next me at table, my fire-lock lean'd in the corner.[33]

Since Whitman, the man, expressed the belief in "The Eighteenth Presidency" that the Fugitive Slave Act should be obeyed for the sake of preserving the Union, he would probably have turned the runaway over to the proper Federal Authorities. An equally pathetic picture is delineated as follows:

> I am the hounded slave, I wince at the bite of the dogs,
> Hell and despair are upon me, crack and again crack the marksmen,
> I clutch the rails of the fence, my gore dribs, thinn'd with the ooze of my skin,
> I fall on the weeds and stones,
> The riders spur their unwilling horses, haul close,

[33] *Ibid.*, p. 44.

Taunt my dizzy ears and beat me violently over the
head with whipstocks.[34]

But when the romantic or pathetic conception of the
slave was no more, Whitman found himself undecided
in his method of treatment of the black race. Such indecision can be illustrated from the poem "Salut au
Monde!" In section eleven of "Salut au Monde!" he
characterized the African:

You dim-descended, black, divine-soul'd African, large,
fine-headed, nobly-formed, superbly destin'd, on
equal terms with me![35]

but in the following section his enthusiasm is modu-
lated:

You Hottentot with clicking palate! you wooly-hair'd
hordes!
You own'd persons dropping sweat-drops or blood-
drops!
You human forms with the fathomless ever-impressive
countenances of brutes!
You poor koboo whom the meanest of the rest look
down upon for all your glimmering language and
spirituality!
You dwarf'd Kamtschatkan, Greenlander, Lapp!
You Austral negro, naked, red, sooty, with protrusive
lip, groveling, seeking your food!

You Caffre, Berber, Soudanese!
You haggard, uncouth, untutor'd Bedowee!
You plague-swarms in Madras, Nankin, Kaubel, Cairo!
You benighted roamer of Amazonia! You Patagonian!
You Feejeeman!

[34] *Ibid.*, pp. 80-81.
[35] *Ibid.*, p. 172.

I do not say one word against you, away back there
    where you stand,
(You will come forward in due time to my side).[36]

That Whitman was fascinated by exaggerations in physiognomy and differences in color is evident. That these differences kept even the poet from recognizing anything other than the equal divinity of souls is also obvious. Whitman was forced to conclude that only in due time could he accept these black tribes as equals. For the present, these groups must be satisfied in knowing that "I do not prefer others so very much before you either."

Whitman would not have been worried by the fact that he contradicted himself in the same poem, for is he not large? Does he not contain multitudes? And is not America the land for white men only? And is it not better so?

Notwithstanding arguments to the contrary, Whitman disliked the Negro, could not or would not believe in his ability to progress, and saw no place for him in America or the America to come. Basically, he never accepted the free Negro. Whitman referred to the Negro almost constantly as "nigger" or "darky." He consistently refused to give to the Negro a status worthy of respect. Therefore, the Negro, as well as the Indian, must be excluded from Whitman's concept of the native American man.

Since the status of the two large groups of people present in America who could be distinguished on the basis of color has been decided, we have arrived at a concept of America for white men only. Obviously, to Whitman a native American man could be only of the white race. However, there are multitudes of people of

[36] *Ibid.*, pp. 174-175.

various nations and racial stocks designated by the adjective "white." Did Whitman accept all of these groups of people as capable of contributing worth while traits or of being molded into the native American man? Naturally one must investigate Whitman's attitude towards certain groups of immigrants.

The first great mass immigration was that of the Irish, which reached its peak in the 1840's and 1850's. Most of these immigrants settled in the northeastern cities and almost immediately made their presence and numbers known politically. Most of the Irish joined and remained faithful to the Democratic party. New York City politics was strongly influenced by the Irish, and anti-Catholic and anti-Irish violence flared. The Order of the Star Spangled Banner was formed and later became the nucleus of the Know Nothing or Native American Party. Men were persecuted because they were of foreign birth, and Whitman, an ardent member of the Democratic party at the time, exulted in his own nativism. Although he never actually joined a native American movement, his editorials in the *New York Aurora* fanned the flames of resentment against the Irish. Whitman wrote in 1842, "We sorrow for our native land. Having no prejudice against foreigners, because they are such, we yet feel that they are becoming altogether too domineering among us."[37]

In the same editorial, which somewhat heatedly commented on an interruption of a meeting discussing the New York public schools, Whitman asked:

> Has it come to be, that the American people cannot gather together for the purpose of an orderly expression of sentiments, without being broken in upon by a gang of foreign outcasts and bullies, prompted by this fanat-

[37] *Aurora*, p. 58.

ical wretch [Bishop Hughes] and his slaves? In the west, where the statue [sic] book affords no remedy for outrage, the injured community takes the case into his own hands.[38]

The last sentence of this quotation certainly condoned violence against the Irish through, if necessary, vigilante law. No matter how heatedly Whitman felt on the question of separation of church and state, which was involved in the school issue, he had no right as a newspaper man to sow the seeds of further violence against the Irish.

A few days later, however, upon being reprimanded in a letter from a reader, Whitman sought to clarify his position. He "defined" it as follows:

The motives of the *Aurora,* in some of its recent steps, have been much misunderstood. We have no antipathy or bigoted ill will to *foreigners.* God forbid! Our love is capacious enough, and our arms wide enough, to encircle all men, whether they have birth in our glorious republic, the monarchies of Europe, or the hot deserts of Africa—whatever be their origin or their native land. Our mind is not one of that narrow description which confines its good will by a shore or a boundary line; we look upon all human beings as brethren, entitled all to our regard, our good offices, the protection of government, and the enjoyment of freedom.

Yet we cannot shut our eyes to the painful truth that this nation—all vigorous in the bloom of youth, and, like youth, susceptible to a lasting stamp from chance impressions—is in danger of being deterred from a proud and lofty path by influences of an anti-American tendency spread through its width and breadth, and made more plenty by every packet and steam ship that arrives in our docks from abroad. We possess in this

[38] *Ibid.*

republic the advantages and the capacities, for involving
the Great Problem—the problem of how far Man, the
masterpiece of cunningest Omniscience, can have his
nature perfected by himself, and can be trusted to
govern himself. We possess the chance of spreading to
the gaze of the world, the glorious spectacle of a continent peopled by freemen—freemen, not as those of
vaunted Rome, and voluptuous Venice—not free in
grades—but freemen in a reality far beyond even what
our nation now enjoys. We would that all the taint of
time defiled custom—all the poisonous atmosphere of
European philosophy—all the fallacious glitter of a
literature which, being under the patronage of courts
and princes and haughty church, is not fitted for our
beloved America—all the aristocratic nations, interwoven so closely with social customs, as to be almost
ineradicable—we would that all this might have no
sway in the land. These things are not for such as we.
A higher and holier destiny, a more worthy mission, we
sincerely hope, belongs to us.

And now the public can see what kind of *Americanism* will characterize the *Aurora*. We glory in such principles; we would rather use our strength in diffusing
them, than, like some of our contemporaries, reap the
harvest of basely pandering to error, and feeding vanity.
There are among the conductors of our newspapers too
many

> "dastard sycophants and jesters—
> Reptiles who lay their bellies in the dust,
> Before the frown of majesty."

He who chalks out the campaign of the *Aurora* is not
one of them.

Our correspondent also takes it ill that some of our
editorials show "the fiercest invective, and the hottest
hate." It would be affection, were we to pretend not to
understand what are the instances alluded to. We are

well aware that we used strong language; we *meant* to. Though professing to be by no means of excitable temperament—we are ever roused to the utmost, by any such conduct as this of the dastardly Hughes, and his kindred fanatical demagogues. The farthest stretch of condemnation cannot go too far against any proceedings which put in jeopardy the soundness and purity of the elective franchise.[39]

If Whitman had attempted through his editorials to teach both native Americans and foreigners the theory that he outlined in the first half of this quotation, then his work as a newspaper man would have been profound indeed. However, Whitman lapsed constantly into invective and could not avoid doing so even in the last paragraph of this definition of his position. A new race of freemen was to be developed, Whitman felt, but Whitman had no notions as to how the actual development would take place. In the meantime, he resented any change that might come from outside the United States or the introduction of any old-world ideas or customs. Consequently, Whitman fought the Irish in one issue of his paper, and denied that he had any prejudices against foreigners in an issue or two later. For example, the *Aurora* editorial for April 7, 1842 denied that the editor held any prejudices against foreigners:

Again, from our inmost hearts, we thank our countrymen. Our *countrymen!* the phrase rolls pleasantly from our tongue. We glory in being *true Americans*. And we profess to impress *Aurora* with the same spirit. We have taken high American ground—not the ground of exclusiveness, of partiality, of bigoted bias against those whose birthplace is three thousand miles from our own

[39] *Ibid.*, pp. 63-64.

—but based upon a desire to possess the republic of a proper respect for itself and its citizens, and of what is due to its own capacities, and its own dignity. There are a thousand dangerous influences operating among us —influences whose tendency is to assimilate this land in thought, in social customs, and, to a degree, in government, with the moth eaten systems of the old world. *Aurora* is imbued with a deadly hatred to all these influences; she wages open, and incessant war against them.[40]

Another denial of prejudice against foreigners was evidently touched off by a note in a rival newspaper which stated that the *Aurora* had been roaring in behalf of the Native American Party. Whitman answered by writing:

One of the most ardent wishes of our soul is to see the American people imbued with a feeling of respect for and confidence in, *themselves*—a feeling that shall impel them to place their own kind, and their own merits first. Entertaining a sentiment of this sort, we cannot look round and behold timid servility to a factious gang of foreigners—or the fostering, in our own republic, of trashy and poisonous European literature— or the bending of knees to the dicta of old world critics, merely because their commands come "by authority"— or the influx among us of vapid English, Scotch, French, and German quacks—without lifting our voice, and, in our way, doing all that we can to denounce and condemn these things.

It becomes our people to have a decent and proper pride in their government and their country. We possess the most glorious constitution, the most enviable freedom, the happiest and best educated mass of citizens, of any nation that ever existed on the face of the

40 *Ibid.*, p. 117.

earth. It is well for us to exult in this. Travellers, to be sure, talk about the national vanity of the Americans— but we appeal to any observing man if, in our conduct, we do not show a lamentable want of self-complacency, of reliance on our intrinsic worth, and of independence of foreign sway.

Yet with all our antipathy for everything that may tend to assimilate our country to the kingdoms of Europe, we repudiate such doctrines as have character- ised the "Native American" party. We could see no man disfranchised, because he happened to be born three thousand miles off. We go for the largest liberty—the widest extension of the immunities of the people, as well as the blessings of government. Let us receive these foreigners to our shores and our good offices. While it is unbecoming for us to fawn upon them and flatter their whims, it is equally unnecessary that we should draw the line of exclusiveness, and say, stand off, I am better than thou.[41]

Four years later in 1846, Whitman summed up the situation as follows:

The plain truth is, if nearly all which the enemies of the adopted citizens say against the latter were actually true, there are so many other issues upon which to have political parties—such far more important measures which affect the very vitals of the national weal—that this single point of nativism deserves to hold but a feather's weight.[42]

In between these various attempts to establish as his purpose the larger issue of the new freeman who is to

[41] *Ibid.*, pp. 82-83.
[42] *The Gathering of the Forces,* Vol. I, p. 22. In discussing the Know-Nothing Party with Traubel, Whitman conveniently forgot the part he had played in encouraging such a movement and told Traubel that such movements had occurred before his time. Vol. III of *With Walt Whitman in Camden,* p. 93.

arise and the new form of government which will govern the new freeman, Whitman berated foreigners in general and the Irish in particular. Whitman was particularly bitter concerning the Irish for they were Catholic and intensely loyal to their church. Loyal Democrat that he was, Whitman nevertheless opposed all institutionalized religion and writhed because of the influence the Irish possessed in Tammany Hall. He wrote:

> Will the democracy yield? Shall a gang of false and villainous priests, whose despicable souls never generate any aspiration beyond their own narrow and horrible and beastly superstition—shall these dregs of foreign filth—refuse of convents—scullions from Austrian monasteries—be permitted thus to dictate what *Tammany* must do?
>
> The bulwark of truth—the "unterrified democracy," ruled by a tattered, coarse, unshaven, filthy, Irish rabble! Americans, high in reputation degrading themselves worse than the Slavish nobles who of old kissed the toe of the triple crowned? They knelt to the Pope himself; *Americans,* to the abjectest menials of the Pope.
>
> We know there are large numbers of democrats to whom this is a bitter pill—but they think it must be swallowed to insure their candidate's success. In order, then, that a few paltry offices may be filled by "our party" they are content to be thus servile.
>
> But we *cannot* think the democratic voters will be led by the nose in this manner. Let them act as *men*—come out, as American patriots, and defy the priest Hughes to do his worst. He and his allowed to sway political elections?

> "Rather than so, come fate into the list
> And champion me to th'utterance."

It were better that all should be lost, than such a precedent established. The foreign riffraff once yielded to in this case, and there will be no end to their demands and their insolence. Now is the crisis. If Tammany bends, she breaks. Democracy, instead of remaining a term of honor—will be but another word to signify the rule of hypocritical monks, reverend traitors who steal the livery of the court of heaven to serve the devil in.[43]

A few days earlier on April 1, 1842, he had written:

The democratic party is far from *unfriendly* to foreigners. While the federalists of former times, and "National Republicans" of a later date, have obstinately persisted in refusing to acknowledge the claims of adopted citizens to the elective franchise, Tammany has stood forth, their bold and eloquent champion. And this has been because democracy, in its true practice, acknowledges the great universality of rights, and all men's claims to the blessings of government.[44]

A rather clear-cut instance of how far Whitman would go in defending native Americans against the Catholic Irish can be seen by comparing the following rather long editorial discussing an anti-Irish flare-up and the "correct" facts given by Rubin and Brown in the notes to *Walt Whitman of the New York Aurora* since the editorial demonstrated that Whitman was not hesitant in "interpreting" news to fit his own point of view:

A very incorrect idea has gone abroad with respect to the degree of guilt attributable to certain parties in the riots of last Tuesday. We have carefully gleaned from authentic sources and from eye witnesses, a history of

[43] *Ibid.*, pp. 67-68.
[44] *Ibid.*, pp. 66-67.

the whole affair, which may be relied on as giving the right view of the case.

About the middle of the afternoon, a squad of tipsy fellows, Yankee Sullivan, Ford, and several Spartans, came down the Bowery, followed by a long string of boys, and some large idlers, attracted probably by the expectation of seeing "fun." They shaped their course for the Sixth Ward Hotel, and when arrived there, amused themselves with getting into a squabble with some Irishmen, (one party as much to blame as the other,) whom they thrashed, and then allowed to escape. After this, Yankee Sullivan and the Spartans strolled off in another direction, little thinking of the events that were going to follow.

In the meantime, the exasperated Irish retreated to their homes and neighborhoods, gathered over a hundred of their countrymen, armed with blugeons, [sic] sticks of cordwood, &c., and returned to the field of their late rout. Finding the victors gone, they marched up and down Centre street, wreaking vengeance on every person whose appearance or conduct they took a fancy to dislike. No one dared oppose them. Their shouts and howls were perfectly terrific; and we are told the residents in that quarter of the town expected every second to see devastation commence upon their dwellings and their families.

Things went on in this way for a couple of hours, when the Spartans, hearing, in some distant parts of the city, of what was being transacted, and, no doubt, feeling ripe for a little mischief, returned and showed signs of fight. The Irish drew up a threatening front, but so indignant were the Americans who had been witnessing the outrageous insolence of these foreign rowdies, that they joined with the Spartans, and turning heartily to, the enemy was completely demolished a second time.

The Irish fled and entrenching themselves in the houses in the neighborhood, still kept up the fight by throwing down stones, blocks, and other missiles upon the heads of their pursuers. The Spartans, determined to make the lesson a complete one, burst in the doors, dragged out their antagonists, and cracked their heads.

Much sympathy has been thrown away upon the defeated party. The fact is, they brought on their own punishment by their bravado and by themselves being the attackers. We have no disposition to palliate rows or rowdies—but as far as the Spartans and the other American citizens were concerned in the affair, we can see nothing in their conduct to condemn.[45]

Rubin and Brown stated:

Whitman's profession of having obtained the "authentic" details for this article is not exactly honest. William Cullen Bryant's *Evening Post*, which had counseled conciliation and restraint in the school controversy, in an article on April 13, said that the election riots started in the sixth ward when a group of Spartans upset ballot boxes in which Whig votes were kept. Then the band went to the eleventh, thirteenth, and seventh wards. The Irish armed themselves and paraded up and down to defend the polls. When they encountered the Spartans, fights resulted, especially at the Sixth Ward Hotel. The *Post* blamed the riots on the "inflammatory appeals which have lately been addressed to vulgar prejudices from certain presses and pulpits." Besides the *Aurora*, the *Herald*, James Gordon Bennett's paper, and the *Commercial Advertiser*, published by W. L. Stone, were accused by Bishop Hughes of being instigators of the rioting mobs.[46]

After reading the two preceding selections, one can be sure that Whitman expressed his heartfelt convictions when he wrote:

[45] *Ibid.*, pp. 79-80.
[46] *Ibid.*, p. 143.

For our own part, we confess that while our philanthropy is wide enough to take in all nations, grades, and sects, the love nearest and closest to our heart is reserved for *our own beloved republic, and for our own free born American* citizen.[47]

It is possible that if the Irish had not been Catholic, Whitman would not have been so violent in his objections to their being here, but inasmuch as they were, they were despicable in Whitman's eyes. Even though he cared little for institutionalized religion as a whole, he especially disliked the Catholic religion. The group of editorials in *Walt Whitman of the New York Aurora* is marked by Whitman's vilification of the Catholics. His main objection to the Catholic church was its hierarchical structure and hereditary descent.

In past years men aggregated themselves into societies, churches, and associations, honoring the central authority of their organisation without particular reference to the individuality of the persons who for the time being exercised that authority. The same thing we see now not only in all despotic countries, but in all venerable and highly centralised associations which have come down to this age and country, such for instance as the Catholic church and Episcopal church. Here we find honor bestowed in much the same degree, and respect paid to several successive occupants of a position, for the sake of the position itself, and irrespective of the qualities or deserts of the individual occupying it.[48]

Contrarily, Whitman believed,

The mission of the age, as many people consider it is to correct this tendency—to discourage any man or

[47] *Ibid.,* p. 75.
[48] *I Sit and Look Out,* p. 84.

woman from pinning his faith and confidence blindly and unreflectingly to any central authority whatever.[49]

Traubel recorded Whitman as saying:

"I have not been without friends even among the Catholics. I have had friends in the priesthood—half a dozen of them. So far as concerns the Catholic church, however, I have had in the main to look at it from the outside—I have seen a little of its pageantry and read with deep interest of the royal, gorgeous, superb displays in the cathedrals, especially those down in Rome —in St. Peter's. It is grand, grand—O how grand! Yet it has one defect: it lacks simplicity—it has deferred too much to certain sensational elements in its history and environment. I could tell you of a wonderful experience—of a related but dissimilar experience—of an incident in which all the integers were simple—were more directly related to life. It was in Washington, during the war, in one of the wards of a hospital—a poor room, with cheaper furniture than this you see in my parlor, which is poor enough: a three legged stool for an altarpiece—no light but the light of a candle: then a priest came and administered the sacrament to a poor soldier. The room was spare, blank—no furnishings: the hearers in the other beds seemed altogether incredulous or else altogether convinced: there was a suspicion of quackery, humbuggery, in the whole performance: no one among the observers except myself perhaps was respectful. I stood aside and watched, aroused in places to sympathy, though mainly impressed by the spectacular features of the event—by its human emotional features."[50]

Whitman then recounted a scene of soldiers returning from battle, their ranks thinned, their faces worn

[49] *Ibid.*, pp. 84-85.
[50] Traubel, Vol. I, pp. 142-143.

and emaciated, but with their hearts true, as a scene that commanded real worship on one's real knees.

On the subject of priests in general, Traubel recorded Whitman as saying:

> "And as to the priesthood—well, I have nothing against the priesthood except my general objection to any class as a class. The priests—Protestant, Catholic, secular, I don't care which—don't study man as though they were themselves men but as though they were themselves priests. Now, I never object to a man—but I object to a priest—any kind of a priest. The instant a priest becomes a man I am on his side—I no longer oppose him."[51]

This criticism seems to be much milder than the criticism dealt out by Whitman in his younger days. Yet, it still can be said that while Whitman objected to all institutionalized religion, he felt the Catholic Church to be the most institutionalized. The same objections which were expressed vociferously in 1842 are expressed more calmly in 1888.

But not all the great immigrant groups were subjected to scathing criticism. One large group, the Germans, found favor with Whitman. Generally speaking, he liked the Germans. Describing a Sunday in the Sixteenth Ward, he wrote,

> Taking a walk upward from the more staid and demure 13th, you soon arrive at the boundary line of the 16th ward—9th street—but Dutchtown does not comprise the whole of the 16th ward, and you pursue your way some four or five blocks further before you arrive at the "real genuine original" Dutchtown. Once there, you cannot mistake the place—the innumerable lager bier shops, the promenading groups, the harmonious

[51] *Ibid.*, p. 144.

strains issuing from latticed gardens and curtained halls, the "sweet German accent"—all bear witness to the locality.[52]

The scenes in "Dutchtown" pleased Whitman and later in the same selection he wrote:

Standing at one point, we perceived 7 churches, 1 school house, 1 engine house, 1 bucket house, and 2 bier gardens, all within hailing distance of each other. The Germans are a rational, social and happy people; and no matter how crowded one of their bier gardens may be, everyone attends to his own affairs.[53]

On another occasion Whitman remarked:

Among the Germans Saturday and Sunday nights are marked by a little more than usual jollity. That hard-working and sensible people enjoy themselves after their own moderate fashion once a week, and we should like to know exceedingly who better earn the right.[54]

The Germans were a Teutonic people who appealed to Whitman's sense of moderation. Since they could be spoken of as basically of Anglo-Saxon stock, Whitman was ready to welcome them as worthy assets to America and capable of becoming a part of the native American man. Yet only the following sketch is needed to show that there was some limitation to any acceptance Whitman made:

Beggar-women with bad faces and a counterfeited sorrow in their hypocritical, twisted features, set on the doorsteps; on some few well-known corners you may see gamblers—whisker'd, down-looking, debauched villains loafing all the afternoon; a man with a staring red

[52] *I Sit and Look Out,* pp. 131-132.
[53] *Ibid.,* p. 133.
[54] *Ibid.,* p. 150.

umbrella containing advertisements, trudges up and down; dirty looking German Jews, with a glass box on their shoulders, cry out "Glass to mend," with a sharp nasal twang and flat squalling enunciation to which the worst Yankee brogue is sweet music; a small ragged boy nearly lifts you out of your boots by screaming with the voice of a steam-whistle, a wild parody on the name of an evening paper; a band of bare-faced, sturdy, brown-cheeked, hard-featured German peasant women stumps along, escorted by one or two men of unnaturally stupid faces, almost as if they were blind drunk, and followed by "chunked" children in woolen garments of supernatural stiffness, and with no fit whatever;[55]

Nevertheless, Whitman extended the welcoming hand to the Germans as a race.

Two groups of people who can be characterized as "Latin" are briefly referred to in the prose writings of Whitman. One of these groups, the Italian, was briefly mentioned in Whitman's conversations with Traubel. Whitman said, while discussing Browning:

And there is even to me a great charm in Italy, in things Italian, in the simple Italian immigrant, in so far as I can get the feel of the country at this distance. When I got sick that time and went down to Stafford's on Timber Creek, there was a gang of Italian laborers came along to work on the narrow gauge railroad then just being laid; a number of Italians came, all sorts— they lived in huts there accessible, of course, to me, and I, as you may well believe, was only too ready to seize the opportunity and prospect among them a little. Oh, the good talks we had together! We became almost intimate. I found in them the same curtesy, the same charm, the same poetic flavor, that have always been associated with Italy and things Italian. I often read

[55] *New York Dissected*, p. 123.

of accidents on the road—accidents in which the little Italians are the main victim. They are accorded but scant sympathy—nobody seems to care: it makes me sad and mad—riles me. Yes, they are the 'damned dagoes'—always so harmless, quiet, inoffensive. Italy seems in some things to represent qualities the exact opposite of qualities we cultivate here in America: the Italians are more fervent, tenderer, gentler, more considerate—less mercenary: it runs through the whole race, cultivated and ignorant—this manifest superiority.[56]

Whitman admired Mazzini although there is little indication of how much Whitman knew of Mazzini and his work. Whitman's acceptance of the Italians is denoted, and he does enthusiastically praise Italian virtues. But, Italy, of course, is a Catholic country and Whitman's anti-Catholicism must be taken into consideration. There evidently was a place for the Italian's "manifest superiority" in America, especially since Whitman felt that a native American opera would be modeled on the Italian style.

As to Whitman's attitude toward the second Latin group, the Spanish-Americans, the following letter written in 1883 to a group of Santa Fe gentlemen will illustrate to what extent Whitman's attitude had changed since the days when he saw the winning of battles in the Mexican War as proof of Anglo-Saxon superiority and thundered that the Mexicans must be humbled:

Dear Sirs:—Your kind invitation to visit you and deliver a poem for the 333d Anniversary of founding Santa Fe has reached me so late that I have to decline, with sincere regret. But I will say a few words off hand.
⁓ We Americans have yet to really learn our own an-

[56] Traubel, Vol. II, pp. 93-94.

tecedents, and sort them, to unify them. They will be found ampler than has been supposed, and in widely different sources. Thus, far, impress'd by New England writers and schoolmasters, we tacitly abandon ourselves to the notion that our United States have been fashion'd from the British Isles only, and essentially forms a second England only—which is a very great mistake. Many leading traits for our future national personality, and some of the best ones will certainly prove to have originated from other than British stock. As it is, the British and German, valuable as they are in the concrete, already threaten excess. Today, something outside of them, and to counterbalance them is seriously needed.

The seething materialistic and business vortices of the United States, in their present devouring relations, controlling and belittling everything else, are, in my opinion, but a vast and indispensable stage in the new world's development, and are certainly to be follow'd by something different—at least by immense modifications. Character, literature, a society worthy the name are yet to be establish'd, through a nationality of noblest spiritual, heroic and democratic attributes—not one of which at present definitely exists—entirely different from the past, though unerringly founded on it, and to justify it.

To that composite identity of the future, Spanish character will supply some of the most needed parts. No stock shows a grander historic retrospect—grander in religiousness and loyalty, or the patriotism, courage, decorum, gravity and honor. (It is time to dismiss utterly the illusion-compound, half raw-head-and-bloody-bones and half Mysteries-of-Udolpho, inherited from the English writers of the past 200 years. It is time to realize—for it is certainly true—that there will not be found any more cruelty, tyranny, superstition, &c., in the *résumé* of past Spanish history than in the corresponding *résumé* of Anglo-Norman history. Nay, I think there will not be found so much.)

Then another point, relating to American ethnology, past and to come, I will here touch upon at a venture. As to our aboriginal or Indian population—the Aztec in the South, and many a tribe in the North and West —I know it seems to be agreed that they must gradually dwindle as time rolls on, and in a few generations more leave only a reminiscence, a blank. But I am not at all clear about that. As America, from its many far-back sources and current supplies, develops, adopts, entwines, faithfully identifies its own—are we to see it cheerfully accepting and using all the contributions of foreign lands from the whole outside globe—and then rejecting the only ones distinctively its own—the autochthonic ones?

As to the Spanish stock of our Southwest, it is certain to me that we do not begin to appreciate the splendor and sterling value of its race element. Who knows but that element, like the course of some subterranean river, dipping invisibly for a hundred or two years, is now to emerge in broadest flow and permanent action?

If I might assume to do so, I would like to send you the most cordial, heartfelt congratulations of your American fellow-countrymen here. You have more friends in the Northern and Atlantic regions than you suppose, and they are deeply interested in the development of the great Southwestern interior, and in what your festival would arouse to public attention.

Very respectfully, &c.,   Walt Whitman[57]

Although this letter was written by the poet of humanity at large late in his life, it reveals certain Whitman prejudices. The general tone of the letter leads one to doubt whether he really thought that the British

[57] *Complete Prose*, pp. 388-389.

and German stock was in excess. Although Whitman listed good characteristics that could be identified with the Spanish, he immediately proceeded to destroy the effect of that list with his parenthetical reference to the gothic romance type of Spaniard. It is to be remembered that the Spanish are predominantly Catholic and such a characterization would not have occurred to any other notable writer on the occasion of this letter unless he had had basic anti-Catholic prejudices. Thus, Whitman's religious prejudices forced him to reveal unconsciously his limited acceptance of the Spanish.

Moreover, the discussion of the Indian does not contradict Whitman's previously stated views. The paragraph does not contain a single positive statement. It seems to be designed primarily to please. Yet, even the conclusion of the letter treats the Spanish-Americans as a race apart. Though they possess traits which will be a welcome addition to the native American man, they inhabit a section of the country for which these traits have peculiarly suited them. Such traits are needed but sparingly in the great bulk of the common people north and east. Even though this letter was written by Whitman the prophet, Whitman the man is occasionally revealed.

It was Whitman the prophet or Whitman the poet, exclusively who gave utterance to such statements as these concerning general immigration:

> How, then, can any man with a heart in his breast, begrudge the coming of Europe's needy ones, to the plentiful storehouse of the New World? It is unjust to mankind—insulting to the great Common Father of all men—to denounce and proscribe the people of the crowded East, who take a portion of what there is so much and to spare![58]

[58] *The Gathering of the Forces*, Vol. I, p. 18.

Again,

> America must welcome all—Chinese, Irish, German, pauper or not, criminal or not—all, all, without exceptions: become an asylum for all who choose to come. We have drifted away from this principle temporarily but time will bring us back. . . . America is not for special types, for the castes, but for the great mass of people—the vast, surging, hopeful army of workers. Dare we deny them a home—close the doors in their face—take possession of all and fence it in and then sit down satisfied with our system—convinced that we have solved our problem? I for my part refuse to connect America with such a failure—such a tragedy, for tragedy it would be.[59]

Whitman had forgotten the part he played in stirring up resentment against the Irish and other foreigners in the 1840's, but one gets another glimmering of Whitman the man in such a fragmentary note as this:

> In America the dangers are, (or shall I say, have been?) from the existence of Slavery Slaves, own'g noth'g, & from the huge collections of ignorant and non-own'g persons, generally immigrants, in the great cities.[60]

That Whitman, as far as possible, ignored the foreign element in the nation's population is best evidenced in his discussion of the army during the Civil War. On one occasion, he wrote, "I had an idea before I left Brooklyn that our army had at least a large proportion of foreign born soldiers. What it has of that kind seems to me to amount to little or nothing."[61]

Even if Whitman did not here discount the large numbers of Negroes who fought honorably and well,

[59] Traubel, Vol. II, pp. 34-35.
[60] *Faint Clews*, p. 67.
[61] *Uncollected*, Vol. II, p. 28.

he did discount his own accounts of heroism by foreign soldiers contained in the case histories in *Specimen Days*. Many of the soldiers, he there leads the reader to believe, got off the boat and joined the army. In 1888, Whitman gave Traubel a letter expressing the following views:

> I have been here and in front nine months doing this thing and have learned much—the soldiers are from fifteen to twenty-five or six years of age—lads of fifteen or sixteen more frequent than you have any idea—seven-eighths of the army are Americans, our own stock—the foreign element in the army is much overrated and is of not much account anyhow. There are no hospitals (there are dozens of them in and around Washington) you must understand like the diseased half-foreign collections under the name common at all times in cities—in these here, the noblest cleanest stock I think of the world, and the most precious.[62]

The "noblest cleanest stock" of the world was, of course, free from foreign taint or false strains that might have been gained through mixing with anything other than Anglo-Saxon stock. If these ideas were not ones that Whitman wished preserved, it is reasonable to assume that he would not have given the letter in which they were contained to Traubel, since he knew Traubel was collecting Whitmania.

The real key-note to Whitman's attitude toward immigrants is found in these lines from "By Blue Ontario's Shore":

Underneath all, Nativity,
I swear I will stand by my own nativity, pious or
   impious so be it:

[62] Traubel, Vol. I, p. 198.

I swear I am charm'd with nothing except nativity,
Men, women, cities, nations; are only beautiful from
   nativity.[63]

Hence, it is easy to understand Whitman's almost complete relegation of the immigrant to catalogue material in *Leaves of Grass*. Even in "Song of Myself" the immigrant is summed up in the line, "Pleased with the native and pleased with the foreign, pleas'd with the new and old."[64] His nativism is further expressed in the following lines:

America, curious toward foreign characters, stands by
   its own at all hazards,
Stands, removed, spacious, composite, sound, initiates
   the true use of precedents,
Does not repel them or the past or what they have
   produced under their forms,
Takes the lesson with calmness, perceives the corpse
   slowly borne from the house,
Perceives that it waits a little while in the door, that it
   was fittest for its days,
That its life has descended to the stalwart and well-
   shaped heir who approaches,
And that he shall be fittest for his days.[65]

Whitman did not realize until late in his life that a full culture cannot be developed from nothing, but that the American culture must accept and in many instances, reshape the cultural gifts of many lands. He feared that the various immigrant groups would be reluctant to put aside their previous forms of culture, but he did not realize that any failure to attempt immediately to begin shaping the new arrival into an Amer-

[63] *Leaves of Grass*, p. 110.
[64] *Ibid.*, p. 77.
[65] *Ibid.*, p. 110.

ican made the immigrant's hold on the culture he knew
more tenacious. In later years, Whitman was to emphasize the fact that American culture would be distinguished by its emphasis on the common man.

Meanwhile, the poem "Old Ireland" offers an interesting study in Whitman's attempt to speak of a land
from which a large group of immigrants had come.

> Yet a word ancient mother,
> You need crouch there no longer on the cold ground
>   with forehead between your knees
> O you need not sit there veil'd in your old white hair
>   so dishevel'd
> For know you the one you mourn is not in that grave,
> It was an illusion, the son you mourn is not in that
>   grave,
> The Lord is not dead, but he is risen again young and
>   strong in another country,
> Even while you wept there by your fallen harp by the
>   grave,
> The wind's favor'd and the sea sail'd it,
> And now with rosy and new blood,
> Moves to-day in a new country.[66]

What is celebrated here really is the rebirth of the
liberty which had been killed in Ireland in the new
country, America. The inference that the liberty-loving
Irish might have come to America seeking liberty and
were therefore excellent material for the creation of the
new average man might be drawn from this poem. This
view is, however, contrary to opinions implied in Whitman's prose works.

Therefore, although America must welcome all to her
shores, America and Walt Whitman will stand aside,
cool and composed, until the immigrants thus coolly

[66] *Ibid.*, p. 138.

welcomed prove that they bring extraordinary gifts or until they produce children on American soil who can claim nativity. But being a native will not be enough unless the children are of Anglo-Saxon stock. Apparently Whitman as a man never swerved from his belief that the native American common man was the Anglo-Saxon freeholder. Thus Whitman can hardly be proclaimed as a believer in America as a great melting pot. Rather, Whitman expected a new climate, a new theory of government, and a new culture to shape the Anglo-Saxon stock into a new type of man. That a new type had been developed to some extent is illustrated by the fact that Whitman believed American poverty, degradation, filth, and horror were foreign importations—mainly confined to the foreign populations even when the occupations the foreigners held were not menial.[67] Without doubt, a superior race of people, speaking the greatest of all languages, the Anglo-Saxon tongue, English, was being born.

Since America cannot be a nation of men only, women must rise to fill the proper place created for them. These women will be, naturally, of the same racial stock as the men or the future soundness of the race will be imperiled. Very early in his newspaper career, Whitman turned his attention to the education and development of women, for America must produce a new type of woman as well as a new type of man. Whitman felt that women must be educated but that that education should be of a special kind. He wrote in 1857:

> The majority of people do not want their daughters to be trained to become authoresses and poets; but only that they may receive sufficient education to serve

[67] Traubel, Vol. II, p. 177.

as the basis of life-long improvement and self-cultiva-
tion, and which will qualify them to become good and
intelligent wives and mothers.[68]

To be sure that women got the best education, free
from temptations, since women were generally weak,
he advocated home education.

It is wrong as the records will show, to expose those
impressible intellects to the miscellaneous associations
of one of those caravanseras, denominated boarding
schools. What is learned there is superficial in the
extreme, at the best, and never can compensate for
the lack of genuine home culture, with its conservative
influences.

Educate them at home. In that way they will keep
clear of many temptations.

No one who has been exposed to the influence of
these places can doubt for a moment that their effects
are injurious. No one who has been an inmate of one
of them can hesitate, for a moment, in considering
them as superficial in the extreme and injurious to the
mind of youth.

All the elements which go to make up the home life
are sadly lacking in the education of our young girls.
A little superficial and artificial book-learning and all
is done. A thousand evil influences are brought to bear
upon them, and those who do not succumb must necessarily possess minds strong beyond the generality of
woman-kind.

The influences of a home education that surround
the recipient are pure—the salutary effects of home
culture are beyond dispute, and in every way it is
right and proper.[69]

Although Whitman spoke of educating women, it is
not to be assumed that he firmly advocated the thorough

[68] *I Sit and Look Out*, pp. 53-54.
[69] *Ibid.*, pp. 55-56.

intellectual development of women. Even though he felt that women were equally as capable as men in certain intellectual matters, his firmest convictions were expressed in the following:

> We want a race of men and women turned out from our schools, not of pedants and blue-stockings. One genuine woman is worth a dozen Fanny Ferns;[70] and to make a woman a credit to her sex and an adornment to society, no further education is necessary than that of which the public schools lay the foundation, and personal study and self improvement in after life must build the superstructure.[71]

Whitman felt that women should be athletic, too. The American woman must be strong, athletic, vigorous, a worthy companion for the American male. He was therefore interested in the health of women. The women of Whitman's day seemed to him to have been extremely sickly, and Whitman compared the women of the past with the women of his age. The comparison, in part, was as follows:

> Our great grandparents lived to a great age, and never thought of lying down to die, till they had at least reached the meridian of life. They were stout, strong, happy and hearty. Why? They rose early, worked like beavers, and never spent the hours in dancing. Instead of being frightened at a mouse at

[70] Fanny Fern, pen name of Sara Payson Willis, was America's most popular woman writer of the time and the first woman to show appreciation for *Leaves of Grass* by writing a commendatory review. Her private life was tempestuous and her writing profitable. In 1856, she married James Parton, a friend of Whitman's, and later Whitman and Parton engaged in a controversy over an alleged unpaid loan. Whitman felt that Fanny Fern kept the quarrel alive. But Fanny Fern, though speaking no more of *Leaves of Grass* after 1857, never retaliated for this Whitman slap. See *New York Dissected*, pp. 148-150 for a full account of Fanny Fern.

[71] *I Sit and Look Out*, p. 54.

their foot, a beetle on their neck, a fly's foot on their arm, in the absence of their fathers and husbands, they would load their guns and shoot bear and catamounts, and keep at bay a party of savages. How have their daughters degenerated? Widows are few and far between. It was no singular thing for our grandmothers to have three and four husbands in the course of their lives. It is now the reverse. Men have about as many wives, diseases have of late been so fatal among the female sex. Do you know the cause? It is found in listlessness, idleness, inactivity, thin shoes, late hours, muslin dresses, horror of fresh morning air, and to that detestable stuff stitched in pink and yellow covers, which is flooding the country over.[72]

Whitman advocated that women be taught the general principles of medical science in order that they might be prepared to protect their own health and the health of their families. Poor health in the mother could destroy the peace and prosperity of any home.

It will be pointed out later that Whitman thought of women primarily as mothers, but he did not strenuously object, although he did not wholeheartedly approve, to women's taking part in the intellectual life of the day. A woman preacher drew from him the comment—"and why not."[73] And Whitman felt that women were capable of discussing morals and taste. He wrote a note, in lieu of a review, about Margaret Fuller's *Papers on Literature and Art*:

Though some treat with supercilious contempt such works when essayed by women we are not thus disposed. We think the female mind has peculiarly the capacity, and ought to have the privilege, to enter into

[72] *Ibid.*, pp. 116-117.
[73] *Ibid.*, p. 79.

discussion of high questions, morals, taste, &c. We therefore welcome Miss Fuller's papers, right heartily.[74]

On the subject of George Sand and her writings, Whitman remarked:

That Madame Sand's works are looked upon by a portion of the public and of critics, with a feeling of great repugnance, there is no denying. But the talented French woman is nevertheless one of a class much needed in the world—needed lest the world stagnate in wrongs merely from precedent. We are fully of the belief that "free discussion," upon any subject of general and profound interest is not only allowable, but in most cases desirable.[75]

Here, Whitman supported woman's right to intellectual development and achievement, but did not Whitman limit the field when he stated that women are peculiarly suited to discuss morals and taste? Is this attitude connected with his desire for greater knowledge and freedom of sex on the part of woman which would eventually lead to greater motherhood? Holloway summed up Whitman's contribution to feminist literature by writing:

In freeing woman from the political, economic, intellectual, and social restrictions of the nineteenth century, the poetry of Whitman unquestionably was a factor; but his ideal of the sex, based no doubt, on his admiration of such women as his mother, Mrs. O'Connor, and Mrs. Gilchrist, was, first of all, that of a domestic and devoted wife and mother. Brilliant women like Frances Wright and Mme. Dudevant he could appreciate, but he thought that for the average

[74] *Uncollected*, Vol. I, p. 132.
[75] *Ibid.*, p. 135.

woman the true career was to be found in mother-hood.[76]

It is to be noted that Whitman usually thought of women as married, as mothers, or as marriageable. Except as a mother or a potential mother, women had little place in Whitman's America. His alleged love affair or affairs offer no pertinent material that would reveal that Whitman knew much about psychology of unmarried women. Apparently Whitman felt that only in a married state could women reach their highest intellectual and social development. As he wrote in 1847, "There is, certainly nothing in the intellectual or social character of woman that renders her incompetent in a married state to exercise a proper use or make proper disposition of property acquired by her industry, or inherited from others."[77] The important thing to be noticed here is that woman is capable of the management of her affairs "in a married state." In 1888, Whitman expressed the importance of the married state when he said,

> Women are often the silent partners but they are quite as essential to the business of life as the men crowd with their incessant catawauling.[78]

Thus woman was to be the balance-wheel, the stabilizing element in the life of man. What is more stabilizing than a wife and children? Obviously, Whitman proceeded to emphasize the motherly virtues of women and the glories of procreation. His chief reason for his fight for freedom of sexual expression can be gathered from the following:

[76] Emory Holloway, "Whitman As A Journalist," *Saturday Review of Literature*, Vol. VIII (September, 1928), p. 680.

[77] *The Gathering of the Forces*, Vol. I, p. 74.

[78] Traubel, Vol. II, p. 63.

As to the feeling of a man for a woman and a woman for a man, and all the vigor and beauty and muscular yearning—it is well to know that neither the possession of these feelings nor the easy talking and writing about them, and having them powerfully infused in poems, is any discredit. . . . but rather a credit.—No woman can bear clean and vigorous children without them.—Most of what is called delicacy is filth or sick and unworthy of a woman of live rosy body and a clean affectionate spirit.—At any rate all these things are necessary to the breeding of robust wholesome offspring.[79]

The destiny of women, their future greatness, lay in their potential motherhood. In 1888, Whitman stated, "How greatly the making of America belongs to the personality of its mothers—the ever faithful, ever earnest, ever strong, ever brave."[80] Since it was the motherly virtues of women that affected Whitman most, he saw examples of fine womanhood often in strange places. Such an instance was his account of womanly sympathy in a police court room. He wrote in 1857:

Next him sits an old woman denominated in the classic language of the police courts, a "Bummer," who has just gone off, probably from the same cause, into a fit of what may be either hysteria or incipient delirium. The officer runs and brings a cup of water, and it is good to see that even here the spirit of womanly sympathy and kindness is not quite extinct, for two females who sit immediately behind the poor creature support her head and bathe it with pitying care—true women and Good Samaritans, they![81]

[79] *Uncollected*, Vol. II, p. 90.
[80] Traubel, Vol. III, p. 420.
[81] *Uncollected*, Vol. II, p. 11.

These same womanly and motherly virtues made
women the best nurses although the ideal nurse was
yet to come. White women made the best nurses and
after that some Negro women.[82] But Whitman was
happiest with the older woman who had been a mother
and who had settled down to epitomize the virtues of
domesticity and motherhood. He was impressed by
elderly Boston women and described them as follows:

> I never saw . . . so many *fine-looking gray-hair'd
> women.* At my lecture I caught myself pausing more
> than once to look at them, plentiful everywhere through
> the audience—healthy and wifely and motherly, and
> wonderfully charming and beautiful I think as no time
> or land but ours could show.[83]

The women Whitman admired most, his mother and
Mrs. Gilchrist, for example, were of this type. He had
nothing but praise for them. His concept of this type of
woman is idealized and represented the ultimate in perfection. On the other hand, in his prose, Whitman had
little to say about the younger woman. The idea of
comradeship which was to be enjoyed by young men
and old men within their sex was not to find a counterpart in the female sex. Whitman even objected to
women kissing each other.

> A kiss should not be deemed a mere unconsidered
> trifle to be rudely pitched, especially by those who in
> the nature of things cannot be expected properly to ap-
> preciate it.[84]

The comradeship that was to be "planted as thick as
trees" would not include women. Each woman was to

[82] Traubel, Vol. III, p. 420.
[83] *Complete Prose,* p. 173.
[84] *I Sit and Look Out,* p. 114.

be a separate entity concerned only with her family, especially with her children. Her destiny would be fulfilled when all her children had been born. Whitman was disappointed in the Western woman for she had not become a more wonderful type of woman but had aped her weaker Eastern sister in both fashion and dress. Whitman did not really break with the past in his basic attitude toward women and the function of women. What he really did was to emphasize the physiology of women and demand more physiological knowledge for her. He did not insist that woman be granted complete intellectual and social freedom as much as he desired that she be granted all the freedom that would prepare her for finer motherhood. Whitman could admire a Margaret Fuller or a George Sand for her intellectual ability and yet despise the type if she did not exemplify the true virtues of womanhood. Yet Frances Wright, who was a mother, engaged Whitman's deepest respect and tempted him to write an account of her activities. He described her as

> a woman of the noblest make-up whose orbit was a great deal larger than theirs [her anti-slavery associates]—too large to be tolerated for long by them: a most maligned, lied-about character—one of the best in history though also of the least understood.[85]

Because Frances Wright had fulfilled the highest role that woman can attain, she was, for Whitman, a womanly woman.

Even those who have written of Whitman's concept of women have emphasized primarily his concept of

[85] Traubel, Vol. II, p. 204. See pages 204-206 for an account of Frances Wright and her activities as related by Whitman. Whitman might have been further attracted to Frances Wright because of her suffering at the hands of the Catholic Church.

motherhood. Mabel MacCoy Irwin in *Whitman, The Poet-Liberator of Woman,* discussed woman's indebtedness to Whitman by writing:

> And ages hence—when woman's sex-bondage is as a dream forgotten, when she stands regnant by divine right—the self-elected mother of a new race—she shall remember with deepest gratitude the name of him who called to her while she was yet in chains, and whose songs did more to set her free than all the songs that were ever sung—the name of Walt Whitman.[86]

Leaves of Grass extols the virtues of motherhood in such lines as

> I am the poet of the woman the same as the man,
> And I say it is as great to be a woman as to be a man,
> And I say there is nothing greater than the mother of men.[87]

Therefore,

> Be not ashamed women, your privilege encloses the rest, and is the exit of the rest,
> You are the gates of the body, and you are the gates of the soul.

> The female contains all qualities and tempers them,
> She is in her place and moves with perfect balance,
> She is all things duly veil'd, she is both passive and active,
> She is to conceive daughters as well as sons, and sons as well as daughters.[88]

But not any woman is to be honored by being the mother of one of the superior race yet to be born. Such

[86] Mabel M. Irwin, *Whitman, The Poet-Liberator of Women* (New York, 1905), p. 77.
[87] *Complete Writings,* Vol. VIII, p. 58.
[88] *Ibid.,* p. 118.

women must be athletic, yielding women. Whitman wrote:

Now I will dismiss myself from impassive women,
I will go stay with her who waits for me, and with
those women that are warm-blooded and sufficient
for me,
I see that they understand me and do not deny me,
I see that they are worthy of me, I will be the robust
husband of those women.

They are not one jot less than I am,
They are tann'd in the face by shining suns and blow-
ing winds,
Their flesh has the old divine suppleness and strength,
They know how to swim, row, ride, wrestle, shoot, run,
strike, retreat, advance, resist, defend themselves,
They are ultimate in their own right—they are calm,
clear, well-possess'd of themselves.[89]

Such women are fit to be characterized as "not one jot
less than the husband." It is from such perfect women
that every perfect thing comes, for

Unfolded out of the folds of the woman man comes unfolded, and is always to come unfolded,
Unfolded only out of the superbest woman of the earth
is to come the superbest man of the earth,
Unfolded out of the friendliest woman is to come the
friendliest man,
Unfolded only out of the perfect body of a woman can a
man be form'd of perfect body,
Unfolded only out of the inimitable poems of woman
can come the poems of man, (only thence have my
poems come;)
Unfolded out of the strong and arrogant woman I love,

[89] *Ibid.*, p. 129.

only thence can appear the strong and arrogant man
   I love,
Unfolded by brawny embraces from the well-muscled
   woman I love, only thence come the brawny embraces of the man,
Unfolded out of the folds of the woman's brain come
   all the folds of the man's brain, duly obedient,
Unfolded out of the justice of the woman all justice is
   unfolded,
Unfolded out of the sympathy of the woman is all sympathy;
A man is a great thing upon the earth and through
   eternity, but every jot of the greatness of man is unfolded out of woman;
First the man is shaped in the woman, he can then be
   shaped in himself.[90]

Whitman's picture of his mother in "There Was A
Child Went Forth" may be considered the poet's ideal
of womanhood and motherhood:

The mother at home quietly placing the dishes on the
   supper-table,
The mother with mild words, clean her cap and gown,
   a wholesome odor falling off her person and clothes
   as she walks by.[91]

This is the picture of a mature woman and mother—
a picture beautiful in Whitman's eyes for he believed
that

Women act or move to and from, some old, some young,
The young are beautiful—but the old are more beautiful than the young.[92]

Here Whitman paid his tribute to the mature women
and emphasized his ideal of womanly grace and beauty.

[90] *Complete Writings*, Vol. IX, p. 166.
[91] *Ibid.*, p. 136.
[92] *Ibid.*, p. 36.

In *Leaves of Grass* he obviously exalted woman as the mother of men. He made the function of motherhood the supreme function, but he offered nothing to the woman who was neither wife nor mother. Nothing in *Leaves of Grass* can be related to woman's complete intellectual development although there is much that can be related to her sexual freedom and the social freedom dependent upon that sexual freedom. Whitman was chiefly concerned with supplying his native American man with a superb, athletic wife who would help to create the "divine average."

Now that it is evident what groups of people would characterize the native American man and his wife and would conform to Whitman's "divine average," one can understand the limitations of Whitman's utterances. One sees why particular virtues and scenes aroused him and who could comprise his powerful, uneducated class—men and women knowing nothing of books, everything of life. These *Anglo-Saxon Protestants* were the people meant when Whitman declared:

> I want the people: most of all the people: the crowd, the mass, the whole body of the people: men, women, children: I want them to have what belongs to them: not a part of it, not most of it, but all of it: I want anything that will give the people their proper opportunities—their full life: anything, anything: whether by one means or another, I want the people to be given their due.[93]

For these people formed the great average bulk which would make America great.

Quite clearly, the poet who has been hailed in many quarters as the only poet of democracy yet produced in America, actually developed a theory of a super-race.

[93] Traubel, Vol. III, pp. 478-479.

If all who entered this country were considered eligible for membership in this super-race, Whitman could be accused only of ~~supernationalism~~, but this super-race was highly selective, and would result either in an exclusion from America or various racial stocks or in the destruction of a democratic theory since race amalgamation would be limited considerably and large groups of people of various racial stocks would be denied full participation in the American ideological and sociological experiment. It is also notable that various Whitman biographers, the earliest of them probably being Binns, had discovered a relationship between the theory of Nietzsche and that of Whitman. Binns characterized Whitman's theory of racial superiority as a theory of equality and Nietzsche's theory as a theory of inequality. Investigation shows, however, that Whitman's theory is a theory of inequality as well as a theory of equality. Whitman's limited universality, his emphasis upon nationality or nativity, and his belief in the superiority of Anglo-Saxon stock led him to his doctrine of inequality. His belief in the oneness of men led him to a seeming doctrine of equality. It is to be remembered, however, that any discussion of Whitman's belief in the oneness of men leads away from his concepts of practical democracy and practical men into the realms of his theory of a mystical democracy or transcendentalism. Thus, there exists a duality. Whitman's *spiritual* democracy can admit all men—the black race will arrive in due time—to equality since all sprang from one source and are in the same measure divine. From such a point of view, *Leaves of Grass* can be considered addressed to all men of the world and therefore international in scope. At the same time, Whitman's interest in the great mass of people and in the average bulk that was to be developed in America under a new form of government, free from the shackles of the past, but in some measure justifying it, leads to selectivity. A cursory survey of the existing races in the world showed Whitman that all races had not reached the same high level of progress or developed the same love for freedom. Whitman, in the America that was to be developed, desired as settlers people from those races which had reached the highest levels then known. His concept of America left no room for retrogression nor did Whitman conceive of or outline a method of instructing those who did not understand the duties and responsibilities of freedom.

Hence, it was to America's advantage if certain racial groups vanished and certain others were not encouraged to voyage to America. Although Whitman tempered his abuse of foreigners with avowals of friendship toward them in his early writings and spoke of the necessity of freedom of immigration if the American ideal was to be perfected, it is to be remembered that the utterances recorded by Traubel and the notes made by Whitman in his last years are conscious preparations for what Whitman called his "future fame." These late discussions of immigration and of all political and economic problems show a striving toward the larger view. In these works are to be found those qualities which have led to Whitman's being thought the democrat incarnate. Whitman was, by his own conception of his function as a poet, a citizen of the world and a citizen of the United States. The real problem resolves itself therefore into a question of to what extent Whitman allowed others who happened to be on American soil to be citizens of the United States of America as well as citizens of the world.

I was looking a long while for Intentions,
For a clew to the history of the past for myself, and for
these chants—and now I have found it,
It is not in those paged fables in the libraries (them I
neither accept or reject,)

It is no more in the legends than in all else,
It is in the present—it is this earth today,
It is in Democracy—(the purport and aim of all the
past,)
It is in the life of one man or one woman to-day—the
average man of to-day,
It is in language, social customs, literature, arts,
It is in the broad show of artificial things, ships, ma-
chinery, politics, creeds, modern improvements, and
interchange of nations,
All for the modern—all for the average man of today.[94]

[94] *Complete Writings,* Vol. IX, p. 162.

CHAPTER III

Democratic Visitors—The American Common Man to Come

WHITMAN ANNOUNCED that *Leaves of Grass* was his auto-biography and his analysis of spiritual democracy, and though numerous biographers have written on the various phases of Whitman's life, his claim has never been seriously challenged. In like manner, the essay *Democratic Vistas,* published in 1871, has been taken as Whitman's exposition of practical democracy. It has been considered, in a sense, supplementary to *Leaves of Grass.* Although additions were made to *Leaves of Grass* in each new revision after 1855, the message of the book remained essentially the same. After the "Calamus" poems and the "Children of Adam" section, Whitman's most significant addition was *Drum-Taps,* in 1866. Thus, in any edition of *Leaves of Grass,* one can find, to use Stevenson's phrase, the "gospel according to Walt Whitman." Whitman outlined as his purpose, the desire "to see how a Person of America, the last half of the 19th century, w'd appear, but quite freely and fairly in honest type."[1] That Whitman celebrated the grandeur of These States and exulted in the existing common man is fully supported by his voluminous catalogues. Though the work was suffused with a

[1] *Complete Prose,* p. 525.

111

romantic glow, it is evident that Whitman was satisfied with what he thought he saw. Yet, whether he actually put the thoughts of a man of the last half of the nineteenth century on record is a question yet to be answered.

Various biographers and writers have assumed that the lines

> Camerado, this is no book,
> Who touches this touches a man,[2]

are to be taken literally, and that *Leaves of Grass* is to be interpreted as the autobiography of the living man. Whitman encouraged this belief as did his literary executors, Bucke, Harned, and Traubel. This, naturally enough, has led to the interpretations of Whitman as a second Christ, as a prophet, as *the* great democrat, or as the great, sane, healthy, native, American man. But it is evident that Whitman consciously imagined much of his role. It cannot be doubted that he created, dressed, and acted a part—the part of the lover of all mankind. This lover of all mankind beheld These States and found them good. The bond of comradeship united or would unite the Kentuckian, the Floridian, the Northerner, the Southerner, the mechanic, the farmer, one to the other. The sturdy, clear-eyed, native American type was everywhere present in such works as "Song of Occupations," "Song of the Open Road," and "I Hear America Singing." The national past and present were poetized and the national future was predicted. *Leaves of Grass* created an America and an American people that were great and a legendary Whitman that was greater.

The quality that made *Leaves of Grass* more than just an exhaustive catalogue was mysticism or trans-

[2] *Complete Writings*, Vol. IX, p. 289.

cendentalism. It was Whitman's expressed belief in the oneness of men that made the book hang together as a unit. It is significant that the interpretation of *Leaves of Grass* in the Bucke biography is a mystical interpretation. Whitman did not encourage his admirers to seek a social significance. The Whitman of *Leaves of Grass* contained all, comprehended all, was willing to accept all. The chief appeal made by this Whitman was to the emotions. The intellect was left severely alone. The fulcrum was to be the dear love of comrades which would bind together that great array of superb individuals who would constitute the divine average, the great, native, American man.

But events after 1865 did not conform to Whitman's theory. No bond of comradeship had immediately re-knit the North and the South after the Civil War. The interest in material prosperity in the North, which had been fostered by the war, showed no signs of abating, and the various evils attending Southern reconstruction were everywhere evident. The array of ineffectual or crooked politicians preying upon the people filled Whitman with dismay. These politicians had been elected by the people. The America of his poetry and his visions and the America in actual existence were worlds apart. Had the divine average been achieved? Had the mass, in whose soundness and greatness he had exulted in *Leaves of Grass*, really arrived? In 1871 Whitman decided not. The people were yet to arrive. The divine average was yet to come. Whitman surveyed the contemporary scene and fell into wholesale condemnation. He wrote in *Democratic Vistas* in part:

Never was there, perhaps more hollowness at heart than at present, and here in the United States. Genuine belief seems to have left us. The underlying principles of the States are not honestly believ'd in, (for all this hectic glow, and these melo-dramatic screamings,) nor is humanity itself believ'd in. What penetrating eye does not everywhere see through the mask? The spectacle is appalling. We live in an atmosphere of hypocrisy throughout. The men believe not in the women, nor the women in the men. A scornful superciliousness rules in literature. The aim of all the *littérateurs* is to find something to make fun of. A lot of churches, sects, &c., the most dismal phantasms I know, usurp the name of religion. Conversation is a mass of badinage. . . . . The official services of America, national, state, and municipal, in all their branches and departments, except the judiciary are saturated in corruption, bribery, falsehood, maladministration; and the judiciary is tainted. The great cities reek with respectable as much as non-respectable robbery and scoundrelism. In fashionable life, flippancy, tepid amours, weak infidelism, small aims or no aims at all, only to kill time. In business, (this all-devouring modern word, business), the one sole object is, by any means, pecuniary gain. . . . . The best class we show, is but a mob of fashionably dressed speculators and vulgarians. True, indeed, behind this fantastic farce, enacted on the visible stage of society, solid things and stupendous labors are to be discover'd, existing crudely and going on in the background, to advance and tell themselves in time. Yet the truths are none the less terrible.[3]

This description of his own day is a far cry from the lines:

> I dream'd in a dream I saw a city invincible to the
>   attacks of the whole rest of the earth,
> I dream'd that was the city of Friends,
> Nothing was greater there than the quality of robust
>   love, it led the rest

[3] *Complete Prose*, p. 204.

It was seen every hour in the actions of the men of that
city,
And in all their looks and words.[4]

Whitman's beloved common people did not escape
censure though he paused to praise the grand common
stock which had so vividly demonstrated to him its
worth in the Civil War. About the common man, he
wrote:

> I myself see clearly enough the crude, defective streaks
> in all the strata of the common people; the specimens
> and vast collections of the ignorant, the credulous, the
> unfit and uncouth, the incapable, and the very low and
> poor.[5]

Of the low and the poor, Whitman had this further to
write:

> . . . . . . democracy looks with suspicious, ill-satisfied
> eye upon the very poor, the ignorant, and on those out
> of business. She asks for men and women with occupa-
> tions, well-off, owners of houses and acres, and with
> cash in the bank—and with some cravings for litera-
> ture, too . . .[6]

Whitman had, then, reached the conclusion that the
mass of people was not as sound as he had once supposed. The people's use of the ballot had not demonstrated any appreciable amount of calm aloofness from
parties and politics. As he observed,

> Even to-day, amid these whirls, incredible flippancy,
> and blind fury of parties, infidelity, entire lack of
> first-class captains and leaders, added to the plentiful
> meanness and vulgarity of the ostensible masses—that

[4] *Complete Writings*, Vol. VIII, p. 158.
[5] *Complete Prose*, p. 211.
[6] *Ibid.*, p. 215.

problem, the labor question, beginning to open like a
yawning gulf, rapidly widening every year—what prospect have we?[7]

The prospect did look dim, for Whitman had discovered that both the leaders and the people fell short
of his hopes for them. The very material progress that
he had so triumphantly celebrated in his poetry was
working to destroy the democratic way of life. Extreme
wealth and poverty were doing their parts toward
robbing Americans of their ideals. It was imperative
that the common man be reeducated if the divine
average was to be achieved.

Although the hope of America lay in the common
man, Whitman believed that general suffrage had its
dangers. However, under the democratic formula, it
was the only safe means of insuring future democratic
institutions. Political democracy would revitalize the
true idea of democracy and supply a training-school
for the making of first-class men.[8] If a man were to
become truly enfranchised, he must be more than just
a voter and must learn his political responsibilities.
Only through general suffrage could America be sure of
producing intelligent voters.

Whitman further believed that the main centers of
political and social importance would shift to the West.
He wrote:

In a few years the dominion-heart of America will be
far inland, toward the west. Our future national capital
may not be where the present one is. It is possible, nay
likely, that in less than fifty years, it will migrate a thousand or two miles, will be re-founded, and every thing
belonging to it made on a different plan, original, far
more superb. The main social, political spine-character

[7] *Ibid.*, p. 247.
[8] *Ibid.*, p. 216.

of the States will probably run along the Ohio, Missouri and Mississippi rivers, and west and north of them, including Canada. Those regions, with the group or powerful brothers toward the Pacific, (destined to the mastership of the sea and its countless paradises of islands,) will compact and settle the traits of America, with all the old retain'd, but more expanded, grafted on newer, hardier, purely native stock. A giant growth composite from the rest, getting their contribution, absorbing it, to make it more illustrious. From the north, intellect, the sun of things, also the idea of unswayable justice, anchor amid the last, the wild tempests. From the south the living soul, the animus of good and bad, haughtily admitting no demonstration but its own. While from the west itself comes solid personality, with blood and brawn, and the deep quality of all-accepting fusion.[9]

From this man of the West, Whitman would develop the man of the future. Toward this end, he mapped out a program for the development of the individual. Whitman believed that it was the duty of a democracy to raise all men to the highest possible average and yet foster the individual. As a means of developing the individual, Whitman offered his theory of personalism which stressed health and its relationship to future parentage,[10] mental education,[11] religiousness,[12] and participation in politics.[13]

[9] Ibid., p. 216.

[10] Parentage must consider itself in advance. (Will the time hasten when fatherhood and motherhood shall become a science—and the noblest science?) To our model, a clear-blooded, strong fibred physique, is indispensable; the questions of food, drink, air, exercise, assimilation, digestion, can never be intermitted. Out of these we descry a well-begotten, selfhood—in youth, fresh, ardent, emotional, aspiring, full of adventure; at maturity, brave, perceptive, under control, neither too talkative nor too reticent, neither flippant nor sombre; of the bodily figure, the movement easy, the complexion showing the best blood, somewhat flush'd, breast expanded, an erect attitude, a voice whose sound outvies music, eyes of calm and steady gaze, yet

This course of self-development was outlined primarily for American manhood. Whitman wanted perfect conception from good, selected, native American stock, mental development, an unsophisticated conscience, and an interest in practical politics to be the molding qualities which would develop the native American man. He did speak of women, but even though he prophesied that women would get the power to vote and that they would become active in many phases of American life, his interest was still predominantly in woman as the mother of men. He still held up as an ideal the woman who was physiologically sweet and sound, who loved work, who was practical, and who devoted time to music, literature, and recreation. Though Whitman vaguely spoke of the new woman,

---

capable also of flashing—and a general presence that holds its own in the company of the highest. *Ibid.*, p. 225.

[11] With regard to the mental-educational part of our model, enlargement of intellect, stores of cephalic knowledge, &c., the concentration thitherward of all the customs of our age, especially in America, is so overweening, and provides so fully for that part, that, important and necessary as it is, it really needs nothing from us here—except, indeed, a phrase of warning and restraint. *Ibid.*, p. 226.

[12] Leaving still unspecified several sterling parts of any model fit for the future personality of America, I must not fail, again and ever, to pronounce myself on one, probably the least attended to in modern times—a hiatus, indeed, threatening its gloomiest consequences after us. I mean the simple, unsophisticated Conscience, the primary moral element . . . . . . Our triumphant modern civilizee, with his all-schooling and his wondrous appliances, will show himself but an amputation while this deficiency remains. Beyond, (assuming a more hopeful tone,) the vertebration of the manly and womanly personalism of our western world, can only be, and is, indeed to be, (I hope,) its all-penetrating Religiousness. *Ibid.*

[13] To practically enter into politics is an important part of American personalism . . . . As for you, I advise you to enter more strongly yet into politics. I advise every young man to do so. Always inform yourself; always do the best you can; always vote. Disengage yourself from parties. They have been useful, and to some extent remain so; but the floating, uncommitted electors, farmers, clerks, mechanics, the masters of parties—watching aloof, inclining victory this side or that side—such are the ones most needed, present and future. *Ibid.*, p. 227.

even in *Democratic Vistas* he was not able to find the proper feminine niche except in the home. Though the new woman would be free and blessed with equality, she would still be chiefly the great and perfect mother. Such women, with the newly developed man, could form the following community:

> I can conceive a community, today and here, in which, on a sufficient scale, the perfect personalities, without noise meet; say in some pleasant western settlement or town, where a couple of hundred best men and women, of ordinary worldly status, have by luck been drawn together, with nothing much extra of genius or wealth, but virtuous, chaste, industrious, cheerful, resolute, friendly and devout. I can conceive such a community organized in running order, powers judiciously delegated—farming, building, trade, courts, mails, schools, elections, all attended to; and then the rest of life, the main thing, freely branching and blossoming in each individual, and bearing golden fruit. I can see there, in every young man and old man, after his kind, and in every woman after hers, a true personality, develop'd, exercised, proportionately in body, mind, and spirit. I can imagine this case as one not necessarily rare or difficult, but in buoyant accordance with the municipal and general requirements of our times. And I realize in it the culmination of something better than any stereotyped *éclat* of history or poems. Perhaps, unsung, undramatized, unput in essays or biographies—perhaps even some such community already exists, in Ohio, Illinois, Missouri, or somewhere, practically fulfilling itself, and thus outvying, in cheapest vulgar life, all that has been hitherto shown in best ideal pictures.[14]

Obviously Whitman had come to the realization that his entire scheme of a spiritual democracy could only be realized in the future; yet he had not given up hope

[14] *Ibid.*, pp. 229-230.

that such a community might already exist in the western part of the country. It is also evident that Whitman's plan is a plan of building and not of rebuilding. He seemed to have no scheme for regeneration of the North and South but looked to the West to produce a new man and a new woman who would supersede the man and the woman then existing in the more highly settled regions. The western man and woman could come into dominance easily enough if and when the centers of culture and government were shifted to the West. This is contrary to all his attempts in *Leaves of Grass* to point out that one man was as great as another. The loving comradeship or adhesive quality could not be expected to take care of this difficulty since adhesiveness could exist only between equals, and the West and the East would become unequal. Though Whitman believed that certain northern and southern characteristics and stocks would be grafted on western stock, not all the characteristics and stocks of the North and South could be included for all were not readily assimilated or desirable. Thus, Whitman's theory of personalism would not destroy inequality. A careful analysis of *Democratic Vistas* reveals that America was still to be ruled by a particular racial stock. Whitman's limited universality is hard to reconcile with his constant expansionist dreams for America. He dreamed, even in *Democratic Vistas*, of the day when Canada, Cuba, and the islands in the Pacific would fall under the dominion of America. What were Whitman's plans for the people of Cuba and the islands? According to his beliefs, they were not of readily assimilable stock. How, then, were they to be governed under the democratic system? Even Canada would present problems for there Whitman would have been faced with the large French-

Catholic segment of the population. Hence, when Whitman tried to translate his concept of a spiritual democracy into practical terms, he ran into difficulties which he could not always surmount. Whitman, the prophet, might have been able to transcend all limitations, but Whitman, the man, had not yet become the divine average.

Whitman the prophet believed that the necessary teacher of personalism was literature. America must produce a native literature and a new race of writers. Such sentiments echoed Emerson's "American Scholar" and the sentiments of other Americans such as Noah Webster and William Ellery Channing. Whitman considered himself the forerunner of the divine literatus who would do more to shape the destiny of America than any politician, preacher, or teacher when he wrote in *Leaves of Grass:*

Poets to come! orators, singers, musicians to come!
Not to-day is to justify and answer what I am for,
But you, a new brood, native, athletic, continental,
   greater than before known,
Arouse! for you must justify me.

I myself but write one or two indicative words for the
   future,
I but advance a moment only to wheel and hurry back
   in the darkness.

I am a man, who, sauntering along without fully stop-
   ping, turns a casual look upon you and then averts his
   face,
Leaving it to you to prove and define it,
Expecting the main things from you.[15]

[15] *Complete Writings,* Vol. VIII, p. 15.

Whitman stated the belief that he only pointed the
way. It would be the duty of the divine literatus to produce works suitable for America and Americans since
the American intellect of the day and the standards of
literature were foreign. The divine literatus must produce literature stimulating the pride and dignity of the
common people since it was the average man, in the
final analysis, who was all important and who must be
molded. Whitman wrote:

> In short, or, though it may not be realized, it is strictly
> true, that a few first-class poets, philosophs, and authors,
> have substantially settled and given status to the entire
> religion, education, law, sociology, &c., of the hitherto
> civilized world, by tinging and often creating the atmos-
> phere out of which they have arisen, such also must
> stamp, and more than ever stamp, the interior and real
> democratic construction of this American continent,
> today, and days to come. Remember also this fact of
> difference, that, while through the antique and through
> the medieval ages, highest thoughts and ideals realized
> themselves, and their expression made its way by other
> arts, as much as, or even more than by, technical litera-
> ture, (not open to the mass of persons, or even to the
> majority of eminent persons,) such literature in our day
> and for current purposes, is not only more eligible than
> all the other arts put together, but has become the only
> general means of morally influencing the world.[16]

Thus, the divine literatus had it within his power to
influence the course of civilization. It could prepare the
seed-ground, shape events, mold the people, since Whitman further believed:

> The literature, songs, esthetics, &c., of a country are of
> importance principally because they furnish the mate-
> rials and suggestion of personality for the women and

[16] *Complete Prose*, p. 201.

men of that country, and enforce them in a thousand effective ways. As to topmost claim of a strong consolidating of the nationality of these States, is, that only by such powerful compaction can the separate States secure that full and free swing within their sphere, which is becoming to them, each after its kind, so will individuality, with unimpeded branchings, flourish but under imperial republican forms.[17]

The divine literatus would be the greatest force in the development of the mentality necessary in a democracy. The foundation of American democracy was an *Idea*, and the country would become and remain democratic according to the degree of understanding of that *Idea*. This *Idea*, announcing the equality of all man, must be understood spiritually as well as politically. A poetry which was bold, modern, cosmic, must be developed if the spiritual needs of the people were to be met. Whitman wrote of such poetry:

It must bend its vision toward the future, more than the past. Like America, it must extricate itself from even the greatest models of the past, and, while courteous to them, must have entire faith in itself, and the products of its own democratic spirit only. Like her, it must place in the van, and hold up at all hazards, the divine pride of man in himself, (the radical foundation of the new religion). Long enough have the People been listening to poems in which common humanity, deferential, bends low, humiliated, acknowledging superiors. But America listens to no such poems. Erect, inflated, and fully self-esteeming be the chant, and then America will listen with pleas'd ears.[18]

It is the duty of the divine literatus, then to create a type of supernationalism. The proud, divine, upright

17 *Ibid.*, pp. 221-222.
18 *Ibid.*, p. 238.

American to be presented by the divine literatus was
to be the type of man who could have been produced
in no other country, except America. But to soften any
super-man complex that could be derived from such
works, a moral purpose would suffuse all. Man would
be taught his relationship to nature and to his fellow
man at the same time he was being taught to take pride
in himself. The moral virtues would be emphasized for:

> That which really balances and conserves the social
> and political world is not so much legislation, police,
> treaties, and dread of punishment, as the latent eternal
> intuitional sense, in humanity, of fairness, manliness,
> decorum, &c. Indeed, this perennial regulation, control,
> and oversight, by self-suppliance, is *sine qua non* to
> democracy; and a highest widest aim of democratic
> literature may well be to bring forth, cultivate, brace,
> and strengthen this sense, in individuals and society.[19]

The priest departs—the divine literatus comes, for
the true exploration and settlement of this country
rested on the writer who would make a social and political democracy permanent through the promulgation
of spiritual democracy.

It is not the aim of this section to interpret Whitman's
spiritual democracy. Yet it becomes evident that *Democratic Vistas* is fully as romantic as is *Leaves of Grass*.
After Whitman's condemnation of contemporary America which was sketched predominantly in black and
white, he laid the blame for America's failure to produce a new type of man generally on America's imitation of foreign models of literature, fashion, and art. The
mass of the people, who had been uninfluenced by these
foreign models, were not perfect but were at least
basically sound. One or two famous paragraphs of con-

19 *Ibid.*, p. 246.

demnation have usually been used as illustrative of Whitman's realistic attitude toward America,[20] but

[20] The paragraph cited near the beginning of the chapter is one of the most famous condemnatory passages. Others are as follows:

But sternly discarding, shutting our eyes to the glow and grandeur of the general superficial effect, coming down to what is of the only real importance, Personalities, and examining minutely, we question, we ask, are there, indeed, *men* here worthy the name? Are there athletes? Are there perfect women, to match the generous material luxuriance? Is there a pervading atmosphere of beautiful manners? Are there crops of fine youths, and majestic old persons? Are there arts worthy freedom and a rich people? Is there a great moral and religious civilization—the only justification of a great material one? Confess that to severe eyes, using the moral microscope upon humanity, a sort of dry and flat Sahara appears, these cities, crowded with petty grotesques, malformations, phantoms, playing meaningless antics. Confess that everywhere, in shop, street, church, theatre, bar-room, official chair, are pervading flippancy and vulgarity, low cunning, infidelity—everywhere the youth puny, impudent, foppish, prematurely ripe—everywhere an abnormal libidinousness, unhealthy forms, male, female, painted, padded, dyed, chignon'd, muddy complexions, bad blood, the capacity for good motherhood deceasing or deceas'd, shallow notions of beauty, with a range of manners, or lack of manners, (considering the advantages enjoy'd,) probably the meanest to be seen in the world. *Ibid.*, pp. 205-206.

Once, before the war, (alas! I dare not say how many times the mood has come!) I, too, was fill'd with doubt and gloom. A foreigner, an acute and good man, had impressively said to me, that day—putting in form indeed, my own observations: "I have travel'd much to the speeches of the candidates, and read the journals, and gone into the public houses, and heard the unguarded talk of men. And I have found your vaunted America honeycomb'd from top to toe with infidelism, even to itself and its own programme. I have mark'd the brazen, hell-faces of secession and slavery gazing defiantly from all the windows and doorways. I have everywhere found, primarily, thieves and scalliwags arranging the nominations to office, and sometimes filling the offices themselves. I have found the north just as full of bad stuff as the south. Of the holders of public office in the Nation or the States or their municipalities, I have found that not one in a hundred has been chosen by any spontaneous selection of the outsiders, the people, but all have been nominated and put through by little or large caucuses of the politicians, and have got in by corrupt rings and electioneering, not capacity or desert. I have noticed how the millions of sturdy farmers and mechanics are thus the helpless supplejacks of comparatively few politicians. And I have noticed more and more, the alarming spectacle of parties usurping the government, and openly and shamelessly wielding it for party purposes."

Sad, serious, deep truths. Yet are there other, still deeper, amply

Whitman did not lay the blame for America's failings at America's door. General suffrage would assure eventual political democracy, and a general sloughing off of European habits and models would insure an American type of man, literature, art, and attitude.

Democratic Vistas might even be construed as a romantic escape from the contemporary. Though Whitman discussed the contemporary scene, he did little weighing or evaluating of the times and the people. He failed to make a really critical survey of the period. Whitman came out of his rather secluded postwar life in Washington into the active world of reality during a transition period. A war had been fought and won, but that war was a civil conflict. Much of the country had not recovered from that war. A decision had to be made about the status of the South. The North, still flushed with war prosperity, eagerly sought more material wealth. Extremes of wealth and poverty existed, and Congress and the nation were off on the spending, wasting, cheating spree outlined so graphically in Mark Twain's *The Gilded Age*. The Reconstruction period of American history had little to recommend it, but there was much to indicate to the astute observer that the era would be of short duration. What the fate of the nation would be after the era had passed was a question for speculation, but the future need not

confronting, dominating truths. Over those politicians and great and little rings, and over all their insolence and wiles, and over the powerful parties, looms a power, too sluggish maybe, but ever holding decisions and decrees in hand, ready with stern process, to execute them as soon as plainly needed—and at times, indeed, summarily crushing to atoms the mightiest parties, even in the hour of their pride. *Ibid.*, p. 217.

Today, in books, in the rivalry of writers, especially novelists, success (so-call'd,) is for him or her who strikes the mean, flat average, the sensational appetite for stimulus, incident, persiflage, &c., and depicts, to the common calibre, sensual, exterior life. *Ibid.*, p. 234.

have been considered hopeless. Whitman looked about him and took refuge first in invective and then in his dreams for America. Once he had looked around and found the world good. If his dreams had been a little less idealistic and a little more firmly rooted in the soil of practical democracy, the scheme would probably have been workable. But Whitman's whole plan hinged upon adhesiveness. In a country whose population he had predicted would grow by leaps and bounds and whose borders would extend to cover almost the entire North American continent and beyond, the dear love of comrades would not serve as the sole link binding together millions of people. Whitman's adhesiveness was a personal thing which involved personal contact between people. How then could it serve to bind together the people in the great cities? Not even a common racial stock could assure Whitman of like-mindedness. However, the role of the divine literatus could be considered that of the supreme propagandist. People would be molded after the image set up by Whitman.

Whitman transferred the flowering of democracy to the distant future. He saw in this democracy to come the sum of all education, literature, and religion. He asked what was essentially a political theory to serve all the spiritual, emotional, social, as well as political needs of man. These demands on democracy can not be attributed to his transcendentalism and his belief in the oneness of men, for transcendentalism concerned itself with individuals, not with the masses or with political theories. It might be remembered that Thoreau found it necessary to leave society in order to test his transcendental theories. Whitman, who was not primarily interested in producing great individuals, was interested in elevating the mass through a process best suited for the individual. That the individuals produced under Whitman's theory would be capable of being welded into a great mass was a foregone conclusion. Whitman did not even consider that in producing a nation of people, all of whom were firmly convinced that they were capable of being leaders, he might be producing a nation of malcontents. The religion of man can be carried to extremes that could prove fatal to a nation no matter what its political or economic system. On the other hand, Whitman's theory of personalism could result in an average man, if some logical method of procedure were followed. Whitman sought uniformity when he asked for the divine average, and though reformers and revolutionists would appear occasionally, they would be able to effect little change. Such a society would have little or no variety, and again the mass, now enlightened, would be ineffectual because Whitman made no definite provision for leaders other than poets.

However, Whitman might have planned for the common man of the future to be governed by the divine literatus politically as well as morally and spiritually. Possibly he dreamed of a Utopia for writers. It is significant that Whitman felt that two or three great writers could lead America into the paths she had to tread to achieve lasting greatness. These two or three, then, would constitute the actual rulers of America. Could it be said then, that in the future, man would know more of government and his duties toward government? Although he might have destroyed political parties and institutionalized religion, could it be said that he was really free of institutions? Would he really govern himself? Whitman saw only the vision. He did not stop to weigh and evaluate and decide whether or not the vision could be realized or was worth realizing.

Man could be great, man should be great, man must reach his greatest in America, man is divine—these were Whitman's dreams, and he expected these dreams to be romantically achieved. Rather than re-educate the existing man and attempt to resolve existing differences of opinion arising out of different racial, social, religious, or economic backgrounds, Whitman chose to proclaim the new man to come. Whitman did not designate how the best of the existing stock was to be chosen or how the misfits, which existed in the West as well as in other sections of the country, were to be weeded out. The stocks that would produce the divine average would just happen.

While Whitman realized that suffrage had to become general, he shied away from the political problems that might arise. The proper literature would do more than superficial general suffrage to shape the destiny of the United States. The subject matter of this literature was to be the native American man, not as he was, but as he should have been and some day would be. The material progress made by the country was to become only a means to an end since democracy wanted and needed only prosperous citizens.

As has been noted earlier, Whitman believed that he pointed the way which the divine literatus was to follow. How then did he fill his role? Whitman's biographers and admirers have created, in a sense, a mythical creature who practiced all the tenets he taught and was himself greater than the divine average, healthy, sane, joyous, democratic. They have pointed out that he went freely among the common people, loved to watch them, loved to board the ferries and to ride with and talk with the drivers of streetcars. Much has been made of his friendship with Peter Doyle,[21] who was one of Whitman's powerful, uneducated men. But these same biographers and admirers have observed that Whitman's friends among the common people did not know that he was a poet. The relationship was purely personal. Whitman made no effort to help them fit themselves for the new day which was to come. He often recited poetry for them but it was seldom "democratic" poetry. He declaimed Tennyson and Shakespeare, and his friends got quite a "kick" out of his attempts. But Whitman had expressed the idea that such poets were unsuitable for America. On rare occasions, he recited one of his own compositions, evidently without acknowledging his own authorship. That these people liked him as a benign, handsome, old man is well substantiated, but they did not hail him as "their" poet.

The literature of the common man was not generally of the calibre of *Leaves of Grass*, and from his own choice of literature the common man probably got little of the democratic spirit. As a forerunner of the divine literatus, Whitman did little to prepare the seed ground through his personal contacts with the common man. Because of his own interest in the theatre and the declamatory arts, Whitman should have realized, and probably did, that much of the work of the coming divine literatus would have to be done orally before the success of the task could be left to the written word alone. The old legends, ballads, and epics which had shaped the characters of various European and Asiatic

[21] Peter Doyle was a young ex-Confederate Irish soldier whom Whitman met in Washington while Doyle was a streetcar conductor. Whitman considered him as one of the powerful uneducated class and their friendship continued to Whitman's death. Whitman's letters to Doyle were edited by Bucke.

countries had reached the people orally. America had no great native folklore, and the sales of American books demonstrated vividly that the common man was not an avid reader of books about the American scene. Though Whitman traveled among the common people and welcomed all to his companionship, he moved among them always as the man. It is also significant that Whitman's anonymous laudatory reviews of his own work praised the man, his appearance, his association with the common man, and his lack of prudery rather than his message for the common man.

Even late in life when Whitman occasionally lectured, he chose for his subject the death of Lincoln and delivered a lecture that was narrative. He never publicly interpreted his own message. He preferred to believe that those who knew him, knew his message.

Consequently, Whitman did not fulfill his own concept of the divine literatus. His essay, "The Eighteenth Presidency," which might have affected political democracy was not published. *Leaves of Grass* was not popular with the common man and its effects would have been diffuse rather than specific. When Whitman was accepted, it was by the intelligentsia. Although Whitman had done much to point the way the divine literatus should take, he had done little to prepare that way.

Democratic Vistas was, then, Whitman's attempt to outline systematically his concept of the common man and the America to come. Democracy was to be a moral force as well as a political force, and the average man was to be taught his own divinity and lifted to new levels of greatness. The future should see an America peopled by superlative men and women, parents of a yet greater generation to come, all having come about under the guidance of the divine literatus.

He is a seer—he is individual—he is complete in himself—the others are as good as he, only he sees it, and they do not. He is not one of the chorus—he stops not for any regulation—he is the president of regulation. What the eyesight does to the rest, he does to the rest.[22]

He would teach man that there were unnumbered Supremes and that man could be good or grand only through the consciousness of his own supremacy.[23] There is little in *Democratic Vistas* that Whitman had not written before. The ideas on the coming of the divine literatus and his function in shaping the destiny of the United States and the common people had already been stated in the preface to the 1855 edition of *Leaves of Grass*. The moral functions of democracy and the adhesiveness which must be cultivated to bind the country together pervaded *Leaves of Grass*. *Democratic Vistas* added little new. Whitman expressed his old romantic ideas as he attempted to escape from the realities of his own day.

What better expressed Whitman's romanticism and irrepressible optimism than these sentences, written in 1872, just one year after *Democratic Vistas*?

The Four Years' War is over—and in the peaceful, strong, exciting, fresh occasions of to-day, and of the future, that strange, sad war is hurrying even now to be forgotten. The camp, the drill, the lines of sentries, the prisons, the hospitals—(ah! the hospitals!)—all have passed away—all seem now like a dream. A new race, a young and lusty generation, already sweeps in with oceanic currents, obliterating the war, and all its scars, its mounded graves, and all its reminiscences of hatred, conflict, death.[24]

[22] *Complete Prose*, p. 258.
[23] *Ibid.*, p. 261.
[24] *Ibid.*, p. 271.

In 1872, Whitman again beheld the world and found it good. One short year had been enough to restore his faith in the existing common man, to see a new race sweeping on to higher destinies. Without a doubt, Whitman's concept of the common man would not allow him to look at man realistically for any length of time.

Just as *Democratic Vistas* dealt with the common man romantically, the essay "A Backward Glance O'er Travel'd Roads" continued in the same vein. The last edition of *Leaves of Grass* that Whitman saw through the press was the 1892 edition. He had provided that the essay, "A Backward Glance O'er Travel'd Roads," appear at the end of that volume. He added a further note which directed that any future edition of *Leaves of Grass* be a copy and facsimile of the 1892 text including the essay.[25] The essay "A Backward Glance O'er Travel'd Roads" and two contributory essays "How I Made A Book" and "How *Leaves of Grass* Was Made" have been analyzed and collated by Bradley and Stevenson in *Walt Whitman's Backward Glances* in an effort to show the evolution of Whitman's thought and the formation of his final conception of his own work. *Leaves of Grass* was the center of the discussion and Whitman wished to make *Drum-Taps* the soul of *Leaves of Grass*. He wrote in the essay "How *Leaves of Grass* Was Made" which he later incorporated into "A Backward Glance O'er Travel'd Roads,"

Without those three or four years, the Civil War and my experience in them, my "Leaves of Grass"—(I don't mean its pictures and pieces in "Drum-Taps" only, and parts of its text, but the whole spirit and body as they

[25] Sculley Bradley and John A. Stevenson, *Walt Whitman's Backward Glances* (Philadelphia, 1947), p. 13.

stand)—would not now be existing. I am fain sometimes to think of the book as a whirling wheel, with the War of 1861-5 as the hub on which it all concentrates and revolves.[26]

In "A Backward Glance O'er Travel'd Roads" which appeared as the preface to the 1888 edition of *November Boughs*, Whitman had expressed the ideas as follows:

> It is certain, I say, that, although I had made a start before, only from the occurrence of the Secession War, and what it show'd me as by flashes of lightning, with the emotional depths it sounded and arous'd (of course, I don't mean in my own heart only, I saw it just as plainly in others, in millions)—that only from the strong flare and provocation of that war's sights and scenes the final reasons—far being of an autochthonic and passionate song definitely came forth.
>
> I went down to the war fields in Virginia (end of 1862), lived thenceforward in camp—saw great battles and the days and nights afterward—partook of all the fluctuations, gloom, despair, hopes again arous'd, courage evoked—death readily risk'd—*the cause*, too—along and filling those agonistic and lurid following years, 1863 - '64 - '65—the real parturition years (more than 1776-'83) of this henceforth homogeneous Union. Without those three or four years and experience they gave, "Leaves of Grass" would not now be existing.[27]

It is to be remembered that it was during the Civil War that Whitman gathered the impressions, later to be reflected more explicitly in his prose than in *Leaves of Grass*, on the soundness of the mass of people, on the native quality of the army, on the grandeur of American

[26] *Ibid.*, p. 28.
[27] *Ibid.*, pp. 45-46.

stock which was not produced through amalgamation or assimilation but was pure and native. Although *Drum-Taps* and the Lincoln memorials were significant additions to *Leaves of Grass,* it cannot be denied that *Leaves of Grass* existed and would have continued to exist without them. *Drum-Taps* does not change the tenor of the *Leaves* significantly. It served primarily to illustrate the theme which Whitman had been developing through indirection. Before 1860, Whitman had not had the ability to weigh happenings and foresee that the bond of union which he so revered might be severed. Although he had stated on March 7, 1859 that there was a possibility of a disruption of the Union, he wrote on August 2, 1859:

> Every Congressman from New York City and every Tammany man who visits Washington during the next session of Congress, will do his part toward convincing the blatant Southern rights gentry that they must take Douglas or submit to the inevitable success of the Republican candidate. The democrats of the North love the South much, but they love the spoils better, hence they will not endure disunion which would leave them forever an insignificant minority. Rely on it, they will find means to cause the South to swallow the Popular Sovereignty dogma and its great champion. Disunion is impossible, Defeat is unbearable; ergo, Douglas is inevitable.[28]

This quotation from the editorial writings of the 1850's cannot be taken as indicative of a clear insight into the future or of the development and logical following-through of a train of thought. Whitman was later shocked by the war, did his part as a nurse, became enraptured with the common man as he romantically

[28] *I Sit and Look Out,* p. 185.

perceived him, and exalted that common man in poetry and prose. But *Drum-Taps* is not the soul of *Leaves of Grass*. Whitman was on safer ground when he wrote:

> I have allow'd the stress of my poems from beginning to end to bear upon American individuality and assist it—not only because there is a great lesson in Nature, amid all her generalizing laws, but as counterpoise to the leveling tendencies of Democracy—and for other reasons. Defiant of ostensible literary and other conventions, I avowedly chant "the great pride of man in himself," and permit it to be more or less a *motif* of nearly all my verse.[29]

It was Whitman's chief theme in "A Backward Glance" that his book had been permeated by his love of the common man. He believed that "without yielding an inch the working-man and working-woman were to be in my pages from first to last."[30] In America, the democratic averages were to reach even grander heights than those high born characters who had been celebrated by the Greek and feudal poets. No literature of the past, not even Shakespeare, was suitable for the democratic averages, and Whitman had tried to evolve a more cosmic chant for the benefit of these democratic averages. Though the distinctive and ideal Western character had not yet arrived, Whitman firmly believed that such a character was being evolved and should become a part of a great aggregate nation, each man proud, yet capable of obedience, humility, deference, and self-questioning. Whitman wanted to show in his poetry that the "democratic averages of America's men and women" were eligible to the grandest and the best. Indeed, the words "the democratic averages" are the

[29] Bradley and Stevenson, *op. cit.*, p. 47.
[30] *Ibid.*, p. 47.

key to Whitman's whole discussion of the place of the common man in *Leaves of Grass*. Even in this final statement of Whitman's concept of his own purposes in writing, the common man in Whitman's final summation is still vague. The question now is who constitutes the democratic averages of America's men and women? If any native American man or woman who worked for a living constituted the democratic average, would not the term America's men and women suffice? If Whitman's chants were written for no particular section of the country, and were international as well as national in scope, why couldn't the democratic average exist in men in other lands and among the adopted citizens of this country? Even here, Whitman accepted the past only sparingly, and maintained "nativity" as the first rule of excellence and acceptability. The expression "the democratic averages" had appeared, according to Bradley and Stevenson, in two earlier selections as the democratic averages of America's men and women.[31] This leads one to believe that Whitman felt there was a difference between the democratic averages and Americans. The term "Americans" had become too inclusive; a distinction had to be made. American character was still in a vital process of evolution. All that was unacceptable was yet to be weeded out. The divine average was slow in arriving, but he would arrive.

In Whitman's earlier works, there had been a hint of his distrust of the masses at the same time that he exulted in the possibilities of the masses. Whitman would refer to a gathering as "democratic" but nice. The use of "but" rather than "and," or of any qualification of the "democratic" aspect of a group showed that Whitman basically held reservations. He romanticized

[31] *Ibid.*, p. 30.

these doubts by making any orderly democratic gathering or expression of the people illustrate his thesis that the divine average was being shaped and that specific evidences of the American man or woman of the future could be gained by studying the existing masses.

Even in the final expression of his concept of his own work, Whitman found it advisable to speak of the masses generally and to pin his hopes for their proper education upon literature. Both *Democratic Vistas* and "A Backward Glance O'er Travel'd Roads," however, leave major questions unanswered. Through what medium does the common man receive this literary nourishment? What new types of literature will foster particularly and peculiarly American characteristics? How will the growth and development of the divine average be regulated to prevent the producing of an unequal society? Since great individuals who will form a great aggregate nation are to be produced, how is conformity to be produced yet standardization and mediocrity avoided? Whitman left the answer to such questions to be worked out by the divine literatus. He himself was interested primarily in the final result—the spiritual development of the democratic masses until they had become transcendentalized into the divine average. The methods, as well as the actual form the divine average would take, remained rather vague.

CHAPTER IV

Whitman's Position as a Representative Democrat

ANY VALUE that Whitman will have for succeeding democratic generations is dependent upon the degree to which those generations can discover in him, and in his works, the attributes of a representative democrat. Since Whitman proclaimed that he was writing the Bible of democracy and that the working man and woman were in his pages from first to last, the work of any Whitman student will apparently be a matter of affirming Whitman's democratic faith and practice. Earlier examination, however, has shown that both Whitman's faith and practice were either consciously or unconsciously limited. The Whitman set forth in *Leaves of Grass* was a great composite individual, a sub-jective projection, to whom the author assigned his own name. This composite individual represented what the man Whitman wanted to be, a fact demonstrated by his conscious acting of the part of Walt Whitman, an Amer-ican, son of Manhattan, brother to all men. He strove to be the prophet of a new race of men and a new era. He was not as concerned with the individual as his writings would lead one at first to believe, for his inter-est was chiefly in the masses who served as the raw material out of which to fashion his romantic concepts of America and her destiny.

If Whitman had dealt with the average man of his day, with nineteenth century desires, frustrations, successes, and failures, if he had mirrored the soul of his age and then offered his theory for man and country, his work would have been of tremendous value to all future generations. But Whitman did not understand the average man of his own day. His bus drivers and ferry riders were romanticized into members of the powerful uneducated group, and as long as they greeted him with a smile, Whitman could ignore the interest they might have had in the price of bread, the wages paid to labor, or the length of the workday. He could ignore the materialism evident all round him, or he could salute that materialism as the second step towards achieving the spiritual development of man. He could not or would not see that in his age, material wealth, not spiritual growth, was the desire of the common man. The common man did not stand aloof from parties and organizations, for he sought economic and political relief. He readily joined and supported groups which promised him that relief. The common man was more of a Jacksonian than a Jeffersonian and his equalitarianism was a leveling process only. He strove to get his share. He was generally optimistic, but he had known moments of pessimism, unemployment, class bitterness, and racial hate.

Whitman described many of the occupations of the common man graphically and poetically, but no race of athletic, vigorous, hearty, uneducated men or athletic, womanly, spiritualized women such as he depicted actually existed. Newton Arvin noted that while Whitman claimed for *Leaves of Grass* all-inclusiveness, he omitted much from his work that was tragically real and present.

In the midst of so many pictures of work and play, of battles and disasters, even, there is no picture of tired workers in a textile-mill at the end of a fourteen-hour day, no glimpse of over-driven women or children in a factory of any sort, no sudden view of the hell of sweated labor in tenements or of life in the more appalling slums.[1]

Whitman also ignored, as far as he was able, all signs of unrest or class conflict. He would not consider the problem created by the unequal distribution of wealth for any length of time. He dismissed agitation on the labor question by stating that labor must make its cause the cause of the manliness of all men. For these reasons, sweated labor, the life in the slums, the overworked women and children could not be considered a part of the America which Whitman could celebrate. The evils of industrialism and materialism would be remedied in time as America became more and more prosperous and gained a fuller knowledge of what constituted democracy. America's demand for well-to-do citizens would lead to the abolition of poverty. Whitman could not conceive that poverty and class competition could exist in so rich a country as the United States. He believed that when the immigrant groups shook themselves free from the shackles of European feudal influences, they would also shake themselves free from the shackles of poverty since poverty was mainly confined to these groups. The evils of competition were bypassed in his belief in laissez-faire and the complete freedom of the individual. He welcomed the machine and every technological advance. He could not foresee a future in which man could become the slave of the machine and his whole culture become dominated by

[1] Newton Arvin, *Whitman* (New York, 1938), p. 245.

the machine. Whitman offered few warnings for the future. The future was all good; the mass of common people could not fail.

The works of Whitman have little sociological value. A knowledge of the nineteenth century cannot be gained from his writings. The nineteenth century man that Whitman put on record was a symbolic man. The age he depicted was an idealized one. Whitman was not a representative of the age, but "he was symbolic of its expansiveness, its moral conflict, its essential quality of continuous revolution, its struggle for fraternity, its large hopes"[2] to a certain degree. Nineteenth century idealism, in many instances, revealed itself in attempts at practical reform. Abolitionism, prison reform, woman's rights, the temperance movement, and the various schemes in communal living demonstrated an effort to realize the dream of a better world. Many of the idealists had as imperfect a knowledge of the common man as had Whitman, but they were different from Whitman inasmuch as they tried to work out a suitable theory for a better life in their own day. They viewed their world more realistically and worked to eliminate existing social evils. The nineteenth century American idealists were less interested as a group in man's spiritual development alone and more interested in his social and political development which would eventually lead to spiritual development. This explains, in part, the interest taken by the intellectuals such as Brownson, Alcott, Brisbane, Margaret Fuller, and Parker in educational reform, the labor movement, woman's rights, and the temperance movement.

Whitman preferred to believe in the essential right-

[2] Henry S. Canby, *Walt Whitman, An American* (Boston, 1943), p. 341.

ness of things to come. By refusing to base his concepts of the destiny of the common man upon the advancements being made by the nineteenth century man, he perceived the future as a glorious upward climb toward unlimited freedom. He saw man as his own God, the master of nature and of his own destiny. There was no possibility that happiness might elude him. He saw man only in happy relationship with other men. He saw no man circumscribed by a society. Yet society existed, without rules or laws, which accepted the presence of good and evil with equanimity. Although Whitman admitted the existence of both good and evil, the chief fault of his Utopia lay in the fact that he never evaluated good and evil or suggested a method for the eradication of evil. He preferred to convince by personal example and sought to live the part of the American man to come.

As an English critic observed,

Walt Whitman's pose is that of an honest, healthy, proud yet friendly American citizen, free of European influence and traditions, and though he admits the influence of the past, even to a smug appraisal of his Old World descent from Dutch and English stock, he rarely bends the knee to precedent . . . . . . He accepts all without reserve, normal and abnormal; strong and weak; good and evil; seeing himself in all, in man as well as woman, in all races and conditions, and seeing all in himself. And what he demands for himself he demands for everyone. 'By God!' he blusters, 'I will accept nothing which all cannot have their counterpart of on the same terms.' He is arrogant and confident; certain that he is right, admitting no poems into his book until they have been tested by the sun and hills and the sea. He is under no illusions about his mission, and is as frank about his aim as he is about his habits and his person.[3]

Whitman felt that the sacred duty of literature and of poetry was being neglected. He sought to fulfill the role of poet for the people. Although in his earlier self reviews of *Leaves of Grass* he described himself as "one of the roughs," there is little to suggest that Whitman wanted to be taken primarily as a poet *of* the people. He was not the common man become vocal enough to express poetically his thoughts and ambitions. He was consciously the poet *for* the people, striving to teach them their destiny. He sought to transcend the actual and to create man in a new image. Man, the individual, must be spiritually revitalized through poetry in order that man, the mass, might be welded into the strongest and greatest nation that had ever existed. The individual was important only in relation to the contribution he could make toward molding the great mass of men. Although his basic theories were not American but were held in common with various Europeans who were interested in freedom, Whitman was chauvinistic in that he believed that no other country presented such a vast arena for the acting out of the drama of the common man. Ralph H. Gabriel wrote:

Whitman although he expressed at times the sentiment of internationalism, had no doubts about the doctrine of the mission of America. He was always a vigorous nationalist. Although he opposed slavery, he never relapsed into the sectionalism of the abolitionist or the secessionist. Through all crises he held fast to the vision of "These States." When in his thought he looked at America against a background of other nations, he saw his native land invested with a unique responsibility.

[3] Holbrook Jackson, *Dreamers of Dreams* (London, 1948), p. 257.

Americans, as a race, were young. They were a vigorous people treking westward across a wilderness continent. They were doers rather than thinkers. Their philosophy was expressed in action rather than in systems or ideas. The essence of American life was activism. The quietism of a Hindu faith in Nirvana had no appeal to them. They solved the problems of living not by running away from life to the contemplation of the monastery, but rather by advancing upon life and grappling with the tasks which it set. With such generalizations Whitman described his American people, and with this hypothesis as a point of departure he described their destiny. Their mission was to use their strength and their energy to maintain the freedom of the individual.[4]

If the freedom of the individual was to be attained, Whitman felt that someone had to point the way. Someone had to demonstrate to the American people the pattern to which the native American man must conform and outline the destiny he must fulfill. To meet these needs, Whitman evolved his "muscular democracy" and looked to the West to produce the native American man. Since it was theoretically possible for the native American man to come from any rank of society and achieve any other rank, *Leaves of Grass* reflected hope and optimism. It was poetry reflective of the physical and mental expansion which was to characterize America. It was the poetry of the unity and sublimity of American life as a whole. It celebrated man as a group and transformed the individual into a cosmos. Whitman accepted all, loved all, elevated all. Every force was working towards producing in America the best of all possible worlds. Even Whitman's war poems reflected hope and optimism, for the period portrayed

[4] Ralph H. Gabriel, *The Course of American Democratic Thought* (New York, 1940), p. 130.

demonstrated to the poet the grandeur of the country, the soundness and goodness of the mass, and the glory of these states bound together by a sacred tie which could not be broken. The common man proved himself in the Civil War. He demonstrated conclusively that an American type was emerging and that America need not look to Europe for models or for magnificent men. The Union had been saved and America once more had started on her march forward. Whitman's confidence in America and the American people was seemingly unshakable, for he made himself the center of his *Leaves of Grass* and the spokesman of the dawning new day.

Poetry so egoistic might be supposed to reveal the man. Strangely enough, Whitman's poetry, despite the heavy and continued accentuation of the personal note, gives but a partial, a quite imperfect view of the man himself. Whitman tells us so emphatically what he *thinks* that we are at a loss to know what he himself *is*. The great Shakespeare, according to popular opinion, is veiled from us through his extraordinary impersonality. Whitman accomplishes a not dissimilar end by diametrically opposite means; he hides himself by over obtrusion of the personal element.[5]

This over obtrusion of the personal element had led to attacks on Whitman's morality. The use of "I" and the emphasis on comradeship as the tie which would unite one man to another led Mark Van Doren to protest that Whitman could not be considered a prophet of democracy since he confused homosexuality and democracy. Van Doren felt that since Whitman's theory of adhesiveness had its basis in an abnormality, the thesis was invalid for any healthy society. Since Whit-

[5] Leon H. Vincent, *American Literary Masters* (New York, 1906), p. 505.

man's alleged homosexuality was embodied in the Calamus poems which set forth his theory of adhesiveness, Van Doren's objection to Whitman as a prophet revealed one of the concepts of the man which have been drawn from the self-portrait in *Leaves of Grass*. The objection is not to be dismissed lightly since from the same self-portrait can be drawn the implication that Whitman leads the way—foreshadows what is to come. If this be true, a careful analysis of adhesiveness and its relation to amativeness, including the forms that each will take, must be made before Whitman can be proclaimed the leader and his autobiography the blueprint.

Emory Holloway justified his volumes *Uncollected Poetry and Prose of Walt Whitman* by noting that Whitman's "autobiography" had to be supplemented by biography since Whitman made a conscious effort to obscure his own past. The self-revelations in *Leaves of Grass*, designed to reveal a large and comprehensive soul, did not necessarily reveal the true man. In his own lifetime, Whitman revealed little of his past. He referred all who asked to *Leaves of Grass*. The revelations in the poetry were intended to be complementary to the man's personal appearance and to the personal facts which are poetized in such a poem as "There Was A Child Went Forth." The conscious purpose of all Whitman's self-revelations was to teach and to mold. He was the living representation of what the native American could be. He was by his own estimation a native, well-born American. The *Leaves* may be poetry written by one of the people, but the book did not express the people. Rather, it expressed what one man wanted the people to become.

Whitman had no doubt that his theory of America and the American people was the correct one. He had no regrets concerning the past. His destiny was to explain to the people the greatness that he foresaw. It was his destiny to lay the foundation upon which the divine literatus was to build. Whitman felt that it was his destiny to show America that she must produce a culture that would ultimately supersede every other culture in the world. Many of his parenthetical expressions illustrated Whitman's egoism as he sometimes disclaimed, off-handedly, the exclusive ability to foresee the future or to recognize present greatness. These parenthetical expressions were not as modest as they seemed to be for Whitman was not a modest man. There was little of his life to suggest modesty. His concept of his role and his destiny left no place for modesty in the man who claimed to put himself and his feelings on record. But until the native American man became more romantic than realistic in his outlook toward life, Whitman's message was doomed to have only a limited appeal. It was the romantic writers of England, Germany, and the Scandinavian countries such as Rossetti, Swinburne, and Freiligrath who first felt and appreciated Whitman's message. They accepted that part of his message which had an international appeal and emphasized the equality and perfectibility of all men. These were doctrines which appealed to those who, all over the world, were striving to assert the rights of the common man.

No other American writer of Whitman's period has revealed so vividly so many of the varying aspects of romanticism. Whitman's *Leaves* demonstrated a belief in equality, a belief in the necessity of accepting both good and evil, a belief in the microcosm and macrocosm, a belief in the divinity of man, a belief in personal liberty, a fascination with death, and an acceptance of nationalism. The practical man was lost in the seer and the prophet. Whitman had a vision of the future and superimposed that vision upon the reality of the present. Whitman's entire contribution to the philosophy of man must be classified as idealistic. He ignored the base in man and spoke primarily of his divine qualities. His statement that he accepted evil and would never reject it implied not so much the acceptance of evil as evil but as a partial good which could eventually work for the perfection of man. The belief that evil could eventually work for good was itself a romantic conception. The whole of Whitman's philosophy was to be developed by future generations. Whitman's ideas on the future of man were cut from the same cloth as the visionary concepts of a Shelley.

Whitman's romanticism allowed him to submerge any doubts that he had concerning man or various groups of men. His appeal could be made emotionally and the soul of man could be emphasized at the same time that the physical man was exalted. Whitman's romanticism gave sweep and drama to his poetry. There was an enthusiasm and a breathlessness about much of it. The extensiveness of the physical details of the land appealed to the national pride. The boundless energy and self-assurance of the author carried the reader triumphantly toward a new and better world. Visionary concepts could be expressed in the widest sense so that there was no need to work out practical details. Such poetry could aid teaching by first conditioning the individual.

But purely romantic poetry could not do all that Whitman desired of democratic poetry. Whitman had no clear message to give the man who was caught in a conflict between his individual and his social desires.

He had no message for a man who wished to learn how to subdue his primitive nature and develop his divine characteristics. He showed no man the way through his present crises as he strove toward the world to come. Whitman seemed to invite man to live outside his present environment, to ignore that which was yet to be remedied, to evade the indecision that might rage in his own soul, and to have faith in the future alone.

It is this seeming avoidance of the actual, this seeming escape into the day to come which will offer the greatest hindrance to future generations. That Whitman offered no realistic program in his poetry or his prose has been shown since *Democratic Vistas*, the supposedly practical statement of his idealistic philosophy, is implicitly as romantic as *Leaves of Grass*. His lack of constructive ideas and of the social and economic theories of his day resulted in his framing a "practical" theory which was untested. Whitman can best be used by future democrats to reawaken and revitalize the spirit of liberty if it ever shows signs of being extinguished. He asked for men and women, proud of their birthrights, conscious of an interdependency, and at the same time, a self-sufficiency—choosing, selecting, and rejecting for themselves. It is probable that future generations can appreciate fully Whitman's efforts to stimulate the people.

Since Whitman has been a controversial figure since 1855, various writers have attempted to evaluate his importance as a representative democrat and the subsequent value his works will have for any American people. These evaluations have been laudatory, condemnatory, and cautious. For example, Stuart P. Sherman, one of the first college professors to praise Whitman fulsomely, wrote:

He is a democrat with an exorbitant thirst for distinction, of heroic mold, elate with a vision of grandeurs and glories, of majesties and splendors—like every good democrat with a spark of imagination.[6]

Again,

In the life-long evolution of his work, he was seeking a concord of soul and body, individual and society, state and nation, nation and family of nations, some grand chord to unite the dominant notes of all. In his quest for this harmony he clothes himself in his country as in a garment; he becomes America feeling out her relations with the world.[7]

This was indeed high praise, but it did not result from a study of all of the poetry and prose of Whitman. This was a subjective rather than an objective interpretation. In much the same vein, the English critic Selincourt wrote in 1914:

Whitman was poet not of the achieved but the achieving. "Man never is, but always to be blest"; say rather, it is his blessing to become himself, an infinite process. The conditions of life in America in Whitman's time were such as to change a commonplace into a source of inspiration. Seeing everywhere the scaffolding of life thrown up, he too threw up his scaffolding and proclaimed the eternal significance of rope and pole. He rises thus above nationality and becomes a universal figure: poet of the ever-beckoning future, the ever expanding, ever insatiable spirit of man: — [8]

Today, this quotation seems to be a plea to accept the man as he appears to be—the breath, the epitome

[6] Stuart P. Sherman, *Americans* (New York, 1924), p. 179.
[7] *Ibid.*, p. 165.
[8] Basil de Selincourt, *Walt Whitman, A Critical Study* (New York, 1914), p. 251.

of America and her ideals. Whitman's value as a democrat lies in the fact that he was the poet of the achieving. Not until the American dream as Whitman perceived it has been achieved can he be anything other than the voice of that which is to come.

John Burroughs, a personal friend of Whitman and one of his early interpreters, wrote:

The vital and the formative the true poet always engrafts and increases upon himself, and thence upon his reader; the crude, the local, the accidental, he translates into a new tongue. It has been urged against Whitman that he expresses our unripe Americanism only, but serious readers of him know better than that. He is easy master of it all, and knows when his foot is upon solid ground. It seems to me that in him we see for the first time spiritual and ideal meanings and values in democracy and the modern; we see them translated into character; we see them tried by universal standards; we see them vivified by a powerful imagination. We see America as an idea, and see its relation to other ideas. We get a new conception of the value of the near, the common, the familiar. New light is thrown upon the worth and significance of the common people, and it is not the light of an abstract idea, but the light of a concrete example. We see the democratic type on a scale it has never before assumed; it is on a par with any of the types that have ruled the world in the past, the military, the aristocratic, the regal. It is at home, it has taken possession, it can hold its own. Henceforth the world is going its way. If it is over-confident, over-self-assertive, too American, that is the surplusage of the poet, of whom we do not want a penny prudence and caution; make your prophecy bold enough and it fulfills itself. Whitman has betrayed no doubt or hesitation in his poetry. His assumptions and ratiocinations are tremendous, but they are uttered with an authority and an assurance that convince like natural law.[9]

Burroughs was obviously influenced by the personality, pose, and personal appearance of the poet; the democrat of today or tomorrow, supplied with judicious biographies of the man and with copies of his work and far removed from his benign personal influence, will find this account romantic and extravagant. Burroughs' remarks lead one to see the truth of Perry's statement, "It is no wonder that in their enthusiastic personal loyalty they lose all sense of literary proportion, and praise Walt Whitman in terms that would be extravagant even if applied to a poet of the rank of Dante."[10]

More recently, Whitman's value as a representative democrat has been summed up by Newton Arvin as follows:

In no literal or rounded sense had Whitman been, in *Leaves of Grass*, the poet of an international social democracy; on the contrary, he had been in those senses and others the poet of the exuberant, middle-class, nationalistic democracy of nineteenth-century America, and indeed he had given utterance to some motives in that older American culture that were fruitless or mischievous. He had given utterance, however, to far more in it that was profoundly progressive, profoundly humanistic; to all *that* he was measurably closer, in his characteristic genius than any other of our important writers and than all but a handful of writers to all that was freest, boldest, most popular, most companionable in the contradictory life of the age: he had a magnificent plastic power, simply as an artist, in rendering

[9] John Burroughs, *Whitman, A Study* (New York, 1906), p. 302.
[10] Bliss Perry, *Walt Whitman, His Life and Work* (New York, 1906), p. 302.

it all with extraordinary life and originality in verse.
What is weakly transcendental or too simply egoistic or
waywardly personal in Whitman's book will rapidly be
—or is already—discarded and forgotten. Enough and
more than enough remains to fortify the writers and the
men of our time in their struggles against a dark bar-
barian reaction, and to interest and animate the peoples
of a near future in their work of building a just society.
To such men it is and will be clearer and clearer that,
from our recent past, we inherit no fuller or braver
anticipatory statement than *Leaves of Grass* of a democratic and fraternal humanism.[11]

Obviously, the interpretations of Whitman as a
democrat made by various writers either demand that
the picture of the man gained from *Leaves of Grass* and
the book itself must be taken at face value, or that inconsistencies in the man be ignored and *Leaves of Grass*
be taken as the final work on the subject. Both interpretations lead to a romantic conception of Whitman and
his works. Both lead to the complete subjugation of the
man to the poet. Both deny that anything or anybody
could be refused acceptance in *Leaves of Grass*. Both
ignore the particular in the quest for the general. By
insisting upon a romantic interpretation of Whitman
as a democrat, writers have confined Whitman's influence to the intelligentsia and separated him from the
common man. Humanism as a theory would not interest
the common man. The American common man has
never been characterized as a thinker.

Whitman himself favored the romantic interpretation
of his work, since as a poet he had taken a romantic
attitude toward all life. He carefully destroyed nearly
every piece of the work of his earlier days that he felt

[11] Arvin, *op. cit.*, pp. 289-90.

would damage the reputation which he wished to leave for future generations. He was aware that this impression could be changed by bits of juvenilia. The early writings that he wished preserved were published in *Specimen Days and Collect*. It is from the earlier uncollected works that Whitman attempted to suppress that the modern student can find the material which can refute the Whitman autobiography. From these works, Whitman the man emerged. He represented the ordinary, not too well educated, common man of the century, prejudiced, opinionated, boastfully proud of his nativity, suspicious of foreigners, blatantly imperialistic, and materially grasping. Whitman, like the average common man of the age, gathered his knowledge of practical affairs chiefly from the newspapers. That knowledge was superficial for Whitman was not a serious student but an acceptor of ideas or impressions that pleased him. His notes made on his infrequent trips about the country dealt primarily with what he saw and heard. Note how much appeal was made to the various senses in *Leaves of Grass*—hearing, in "I Hear America Singing," "Starting from Paumanok," and "Salut Au Monde"; *seeing* in the various scenes in "Song of Myself"; *touch* in the Calamus poems. The intellectual content of Whitman's poems is often slight. The originality of his intellectual ideas and his methods of writing has been carefully studied by G. W. Allen, Rebecca Coy, J. J. Rubin, F. M. Smith, as well as by other scholars. Such investigations have revealed that the originality of Whitman's thinking has been over-estimated although his debt to English and American writers of his own day and to the Bible has yet to be ascertained fully. One thing is certain, however. There was nothing new about the Whitmanesque thought. The difference between Whitman's concept and nineteenth century idealism in general was the method of approach. Whitman put all his hopes for the development of the common man into the hands of the poet-prophet. He turned his back on practical problems and preferred to live in an inner spiritual world.

If one accepts the interpretation that Whitman thought only of a spiritual democracy and felt that political and social democracy would fail unless that spiritual democracy were achieved, then all that is required of each man is, in a sense, that he let his soul stand cool and composed since in his heart he knows that all men are spiritually and divinely equal. It would not matter that in practical life they may be socially and economically unequal. In such a manner, the good woman and the prostitute, the president and the farmer, the northerner and the southerner are equalized. It would be necessary for the actions of each to demonstrate to the other that he recognized this spiritual equality.

Whitman was delighted by Thoreau's description, "*He is Democracy*," and made a special effort to see that Thoreau's comment was included in the Bucke biography. Thoreau made this statement after having met Whitman and after having been influenced by the man's appearance and personality. Before meeting Whitman, he had been annoyed by the egoism and brag he had discovered in *Leaves of Grass*. Thoreau himself was an idealist who was trying to work out the destiny of the individual. He cared little for government or for superimposed institutions but found it necessary to live apart from the little town of Concord if he were to test his own theories of individuality. Great indeed would be his admiration for one who could seemingly live among men, embrace all, and gain a more complete individuality by doing so. It was Whitman's personality which caused Thoreau to change his mind about the book and the man.

Those who knew Whitman personally were most enthusiastic and worshipful in their praise of his democracy and his universality. Those who knew only his authorized work and the early biographies recognized some inconsistencies but forgave all in a contemplation of Whitman's belief in spiritual equality. Those who have studied Whitman in more recent times have not been able to declare so firmly that Whitman was democracy, and research has often taken the form of justification or explanation as well as analysis and interpretation. If the writings of Whitman do not sweep the reader into instant and enthusiastic uncritical praise, or into instant distaste, the reader is fascinated enough to want to learn more about the man who attempted to make himself the spokesman and exponent of American democracy. It is from those whom he at first fascinates that Whitman's reputation as a representative democrat is likely to suffer. It is for this group that Whitman wrote, "do not try to explain me; I cannot explain myself," in an attempt at self-justification. There is a great deal of evidence to substantiate the theory that Whitman did not understand his own message, and there are numerous indications that he steered clear of interpreting his own social import. But the Whitman student has found that there is much to explain if he is to understand Whitman. One is forced to reach the conclusion that Whitman the man and Whitman the poet must be treated as separate individuals. Whitman, the man, is representative of *a* common man while Whitman, the poet, is a symbolic man voicing bits of nineteenth century romantic philosophy. If Whitman the poet is alone to be accepted as the best representative of American democracy, then the works of those commentators on Whitman who consider him as such must be more widely disseminated than even the works of the poet. Little or no attention can be paid to any works of Whitman other than *Leaves of Grass* and the authorized *Complete Prose*. The Bucke and the Burroughs interpretations of the man and his works must be taken as definitive. If this is the impression that America wishes to give to the world, then the collectors of the newspaper writings and other prose pieces of Whitman have done the poet and America a great disservice. A fresh generation of scholars must then begin to create anew a false god constructed along the lines laid down by Whitman.

Inasmuch as these earlier pieces have been collected and must exert an influence upon scholarly interpretations that will be made in the future, it is necessary that caution be used before proclaiming Whitman the voice of democratic America. It might seem to groups in America and to countries abroad that America in doing so deliberately perpetrated a fraud. To offer Whitman to a world that is, in many instances, attempting to shake off the last vestiges of Anglo-Saxon domination and exploitation is to offer a theory of the Anglo-Saxon as a superior being and America as the home of Anglo-Saxons at a most unfortunate time. A part of the world has not yet recovered from having fought a war to destroy the German and the Japanese theories of a super race. At the same time, although the populations of some countries might remain more or less homogeneous, the very technology that Whitman exulted in has made isolation impossible. Travel, the exchange of ideas, and the need for the importation and exportation of economic goods have made inter-communication and cooperation necessary. The need for alliances to preserve the peace prevents any race of men from proclaiming that it is superior to any other race. And in America, itself, a full acceptance of Whitman as the poet of democracy denies that large segments of the population are citizens of a democracy.

Even if *Leaves of Grass* would first impress for its seeming internationalism and its cry for brotherhood, it can be shown that the author of the *Leaves* fell far short of his own concept of the "divine average" and realized it enough to assume a pose. It would be better, then, to call Whitman the poet of spiritual equality for Whitman accepted the belief that each man has a divine soul. If he is denominated the poet of democracy, the term democracy as he used it should be reinterpreted and completely divorced from all political and social theories even though Whitman touched upon these themes in his prose works. All existing political and social theories or changes must be thought of only as a means toward an end. His interest in the common man must be made dependent upon his belief that the poet-prophet will teach spiritual democracy, for spiritual democracy is the only logical goal. Then some day, in the distant future, spiritual democracy might lead to a greater social and political democracy. The poet-prophet, as well as the great training-school, general suffrage, would have done the job which fate destined. Until then, those who could not meet the requirements for the divine average must find consolation in developing their spiritual individuality. The inner world of the spirit must become so important that the outer world of everyday living can be ignored.

The democrat of the present or the future who seeks representative democracy should consult other sources and assign to Whitman a role he can fill without qualification—that of a peculiarly American poet. The best remembered poets of Whitman's age are Longfellow, Holmes, Whittier, Emerson, and Lowell. Though each of these poets touched upon phases of American life, their works were indebted to traditions of the past. With the possible exception of Whittier, the poetry of these writers represented a continuation of the English tradition. Whitman broke with that tradition. Although his theory of mystical democracy was not exclusively American, there are many factors in his poetry which substantiate the assertion that Whitman's poetry could have been written no place else but in America in the last half of the nineteenth century. The glorification of American topography, the use of Indian place names, the expansionist spirit, the use of colloquialisms, the use of Americanisms, the enthusiastic welcome of material progress, and the overwhelming confidence of the poetry stamp the verse as American. Whitman further believed that America would provide the background for the future development of man. Not a facet but the whole sweep of American life is taken for a subject. The approach to all is general. The diversity of the land, the endless catalogues, the particularizations of occupations give to the work a seeming individualization, but the whole is a glorification of America as America. It is Whitman's use of democracy and America synonymously that has resulted in his being designated as *the* democratic poet rather than as *the* American poet. For American, in the physical sense, he undoubtedly was. The general nineteenth century idealism was superimposed upon Whitman's catalogues or inventories of the land. To treat these catalogues as ballast is to destroy the American aspect of Whitman's poetry. Mystical democracy in general, the many in one, the divinity of man can be gained much more completely from Emerson in America or from any number of European writers. The grandeur of America and the workings of a type of mystical democracy in America can be gained only from Whitman. His political and social theories never really changed from the views he expressed as a journalist, but the social and political failings are hidden in his absorption in the role that the poet should play in creating and transmitting a new and richer culture and in interpreting the great *Idea* to the people. He was consciously poet for the people and strove to create a native poetic medium. He attempted, and at times successfully fulfilled, the role of a divine literatus. He captured enough of the American essence in general to transcend the age in which he lived. He was not analytical enough to interpret his own age and his own feelings. He took refuge in glorifying physical America and romanticizing the common man. Therein, Whitman's true value must lie.

CHAPTER V

A Final Analysis of Whitman

THE EVIDENCE previously set forth has shown that Whitman was not the unqualified lover of all mankind. Yet Whitman should not be dismissed as a magnificent fraud. One can judge his poetry as the aspiration of the writer both for himself and for his country. To accept Whitman's statement that he was the splendid creature set forth in *Leaves of Grass,* that he stood calm and composed before a million universes, that he had truly learned to exclude none, is to make of him a god. To make of Whitman a god is to rob the man and his works of much of their vitality. Only reverence and admiration for the whole can justly be offered to a god. But Whitman's prose destroyed the god-like concept. The prejudiced, often vain, opinionated, enthusiastic man revealed through Whitman's journalistic writings was in obvious need of the benevolent teachings of a divine literatus.

Leaves of Grass was Whitman's attempt to reshape his own life at the same time that he attempted to teach and to glorify his country. When he attempted to live the philosophy he outlined, many of his followers fell in love with the characterization and accepted it as the real man. Since they did not recognize Whitman as a poseur, and since Whitman did everything in his power to have the characterization accepted as the real man, early followers could not examine both the man and his characterization of the man of the future. As a poet, Whitman attempted to exorcise his own doubts as well as the doubts of other men. He fought for his own dignity as well as the dignity of other men. He tried to find his own place as an integral part of America. His spiritual all-inclusiveness allowed him to include himself as well as all others. He wrote confident poetry, but it was based upon a hopeful yearning for the future and a hidden doubt in the present. As autobiography, *Leaves of Grass* was a conscious effort to appear sane, well-balanced, haughty yet humble, average yet divine. It was just as self-conscious an autobiography as such books as Rousseau's *Confessions* to which Whitman objected. Whitman's autobiography tried to create a man who, though imperfect, had transcended all imperfections. It attempted to offer a man at peace about life, death, and the hereafter.

But as autobiography, *Leaves of Grass* falls short. It purports to put on record a nineteenth century man—Walt Whitman. But Whitman the man had been a journalist who had emerged singularly untouched from an age characterized by political, social, and economic controversy. He had expressed himself on temperance, slavery, immigration, labor, and penal reform, but these issues never ceased being purely moral issues for him. These questions, to use his own term, were up in his own day. He was too anti-intellectual to be an important active figure in the intellectual movements of the day, and his relationship with intellectual figures of his own time was based upon the influence of his personality rather than upon an intellectual compatibility. He was not the prophet or the seer he wanted to be. Indeed attempts have been made to defend his views on the

Irish immigration and on the Indians by noting that his views toward these two groups of people were no different from those of others of the nineteenth century or by justifying his apathy toward Negroes and toward slavery on the basis that his grandfather had owned slaves.

Consequently, Whitman attempted to compensate for his ignoring of social and economic problems by declaring that he was a part of everything. He preferred that his poetry be all-inclusive and suggestive rather than selective and definitive. He sought to work for the larger aim, to concentrate on the soul of man. He was not a leader of men and hesitated to be placed in the actual position of directing the fate of a physical structure or organization. He was more interested in being a power behind the throne, a molder of man. Few of his writings were based upon sound logical reasoning; the appeal was to the emotions.

But man is more than feeling, and the autobiography of a man, to be worthy of the name, must do more than appeal to the emotions. If Whitman's autobiography, *Leaves of Grass*, is read by one without previous knowledge of the man or of many of his prose works, the effect can be that which any writer of propaganda would wish to achieve. The poetry of Whitman can condition, can make a reader receptive to impressions, can arouse pride in the immensity and grandeur of the country. It can, on occasion, lift the reader out of himself. He can feel that he is great. But he can only feel. The *Leaves* do not teach an intellectual philosophy whereby the reader can become great. The larger view of liberty, fraternity, and spiritual equality is present, but there is no social or political philosophy which could help the reader adjust to his present environment.

Although *Leaves of Grass* has been called the Bible of democracy, what clear-cut, workable theory of political or social democracy can be drawn from the book? It is suffused with mystical democracy. It is an enthusiastic, vibrant, subjective survey of things American. There is no objective treatment of wealth, poverty, immigration, slavery, or the rise of the factory system, and the effect these had on the American theory of democracy and on the American man. Instead Whitman extended the hand of comradeship, offered to walk arm in arm with the reader. He preferred to sing of the body and of the soul, of life and of death. He preferred to be democratic in the larger sense—in the glorification of liberty, fraternity, and equality. He preferred to concern himself chiefly with the spiritual or inner development of man. He preferred to sing of the oneness and comradeship of man. His autobiography was an idealistic concept of the greatness and divinity of man which offered no practical suggestions as to how man was to solve the problems of living in a sane, just, equalitarian manner.

Other factors limit Whitman's autobiography. The lack of any definite political or social plan has made it possible for Whitman to be interpreted as a democrat, as a socialist, and as an anarchist. Even *Democratic Vistas* was a romantic interpretation of the part the poet-prophet was to play in creating the future of America and the world, and not a vigorous, clear-cut explanation of a workable democratic plan. Although the multiple interpretations of Whitman might each be centered in man and in the society best suited for his full development, the definitive quality of Whitman's verse is lessened by these interpretations. Democracy is neither socialism nor anarchism, and the democratic aspect of

Whitman's work is lessened when any interpretation other than a democratic one is possible. Such a limitation probably arises from Whitman's frankly propagandistic purposes. He planned that the poet-prophet should train the citizens of a democracy since he would be able to do more for the people than any other agent. It was only in proportion to how well the poet-prophet could explain and interpret the *Idea* that bound the nation together that democracy could be achieved. Man was to be taught an *Idea*, not a definitely outlined political or social philosophy. Man was to be made ready to receive other ideas. Man was to be molded into the divine average, was to be made to feel that he was great. Enthusiasm, expansiveness, and an appeal to the sense of American nativity were the weapons. The results of such a program need not be democratic necessarily.

Through most of Whitman's works ran an undercurrent of a belief in a superior group of people. This belief cannot be summed up adequately by calling attention to his belief in the divine average and then failing to interpret what Whitman meant by the term. Whitman made a distinction between the democratic averages and the people or the mass. He seemed to feel that the Anglo-Saxon native, reshaped and revitalized by a new geography, a new political philosophy, and a new culture would form the democratic averages which could ultimately achieve the divine average. Such a distinction was necessary when one remembers that even as late as 1871 in *Democratic Vistas*, Whitman was still dreaming of annexing to the United States regions like Cuba and Hawaii which were composed of racial stocks which Whitman did not believe could be easily assimilated. The non-homogeneity of the then present American population included many types which could assimilate the American *Idea* either slowly or in a limited degree. Such people, probably large segments of the American population, were excluded from Whitman's concept of the common man. It is difficult to reconcile Whitman's constant expansionist dreams with his limited universality and at the same time make him the spokesman of democracy.

Whitman's concept of the common man, then, implied a theory of racial superiority. Though much has been made of Whitman's pride in his own heritage, the emphasis is justified since it is probable that that pride was symptomatic of his belief in his own soundness and the greatness of the stock from which he sprang. A Celtic strain was known to be in his ancestry, but Whitman made little of that Celtic heritage. He began his journalistic and poetic career with the belief that the native American man was the Anglo-Saxon freeholder. There is no adequate proof that he ever changed his opinions. Is it not probable that Whitman's native caution prevented him from ever publicly interpreting his own message? Since he felt strongly on the matters of nativity and the superiority of Anglo-Saxon stock, was it not possible that any interpretation of his own message might have revealed that Whitman's universality was limited? He preferred the mystical interpretation given in the Bucke biography for Whitman, because of his own personal beliefs, and was not sure what his message really was. Caution warned him to ward off those who sought a definite political or social meaning or who followed a program if he were to occupy the position of lover of all mankind. In keeping with his position as lover of all mankind, he sought to fashion a spiritual democracy and was interested in political and social democracy only in so far as they aided in the development of a spiritual democracy. In his poetry, Whitman's limited universality was submerged in his seeming internationalism and his mysticism. A careful analysis of his poetry shows that the limited universality of the prose was also inherent in the poetry. Whitman objected to no man's being a cosmopolite, but he would have liked to reserve the rights of the American common man for a select few.

Hence, if Whitman is to have any permanent value as an American literary figure, the basis of his fame must be reestablished. To offer him as the poet of democracy is not enough since it cannot be proved conclusively that Whitman poetized the American ideology. To treat Whitman exclusively as the poet of democracy demands that the interpreter of Whitman lean heavily upon the Bucke or Burroughs interpretation of the man and his work. Such a treatment recreates for the modern student a completely unrealistic personality—the Whitman myth. But neither the man nor his works need to be shrouded in myths. Notwithstanding the fact that Whitman is still hailed as the great democrat in various anthologies and collections of essays, he was not the representative democrat, the poet of democracy, nor the poet of the common man. He who speaks of Whitman as such must carefully and explicitly define his terms. For Whitman was not a thinker; he was a lyric poet. When his lyrical inspiration waned, his verse became flat and prosaic. His thought consisted of bits of knowledge and philosophy gathered from his reading. The sources of his poetic inspiration are yet to be explored fully. It must be remembered that, in 1855, Whitman appeared as a nature poet. The poetic pieces written before 1855 give no indication of poetic mastery.

Robert Faner in *Walt Whitman & Opera* explored a facet of Whitman's poetic inspiration and remarked that "Whitman's entire conception of poetic art was in terms of music, as he experienced it."[1] His songs were

> . . . . . . to initiate trains of thought in their readers; they were to suggest meanings and to reveal the possibility of meanings in objects and circumstances which to the reader may have seemed wholly without promise. Whitman deliberately sought to awake a "tallying chant" in the soul of his reader, and he even counted on the magic of his reader's voice to color and enrich his lines, as the singer brings notes from a musical score to vibrant life.[2]

Such poetry would not inspire thought but emotion. Its appeal would be lyrical. The best of Whitman does not consist of the catalogues of the American topography and the American worker but in the delicately wrought emotion in such a poem as "When Lilacs Last in the Dooryard Bloom'd." If all the material classified as catalogues were stripped away from Whitman's works, the lyric pieces that would remain would insure Whitman's position as a first ranking poet.

Though he claimed to disdain conventional poetic diction and attempted to enrich the language, particularly with French and Italian words, Whitman used those poetic mediums which best aided his lyrical purposes. He was not an innovator but an adapter. He carefully chose his poetic form, experimented, and wrote. The thought was important, but the form was all important. Yet, a great deal of attention has been given to Whitman's thought since he attempted to fulfill his own

[1] Robert D. Faner, *Walt Whitman & Opera* (Philadelphia, 1951), p. 233.
[2] *Ibid.*

concept of a divine literatus. He wanted to inspire emotionally, if not to teach. But one can trace no clear steps in the maturation of Whitman's thought. One cannot say that the early pieces should be ignored because they show an immaturity of thought and an imperfect knowledge of the role America was to play in the world. All the works discussed were written after the period spent teaching in Long Island. Nearly all of Whitman's biographers have found this period, 1836-41, peculiarly significant, for this was the period during which he loafed and invited his soul, when he began to work out his theory of man and nature and his own destiny as a writer—in short, when he began to simmer. It is also notable that before 1862, Whitman's theory of spiritual democracy and the equality of man confined itself almost exclusively to *Leaves of Grass*.

Whitman wanted to be a divine literatus; he wanted to be thought a seer and a prophet; he wanted to create. But he could offer only a partial dream. The man could not be completely submerged into the poet, and Whitman the man was not all-inclusive, was not at peace about life. In his last years, he saved himself from taking part in any controversy by insisting upon his faith in the common man. All solutions to problems were postponed until the future. He held firm to the belief that the greatness of America was not dependent upon great individuals but upon the greatness of the bulk average which would be made up of the Anglo-Saxon freeholder. He sought only to be the prophet of a greater day yet to come.

In his effort to be divine literatus, Whitman was often guilty of a super-nationalism. The real was transformed into the ideal and the America and the American common man that existed were romanticized almost beyond recognition. But his interest in the American scene did localize his center of interest and he succeeded in capturing, to a degree, the American essence. There is enough of the spiritual essence to attract those who believe in the brotherhood of man and the freedom of the individual, but it is Whitman's lyric gift which will insure him universal fame. His lyric gift led him to search for a native American idiom. His concept of the function of the American poet, his celebration of the physical aspects of the land, his glorification of the body, and the constant presence of man and of woman in his verse were Whitman's gifts to American literature. It is to his credit that he succeeded in being an American poet.

Here is realization
Here is a man tallied—he realizes here what he has in
  him,
The past, the future, majesty, love—if they are vacant
  of you, you are vacant of them.[3]

[3] "Song of the Open Road," *Complete Writings*, Vol. VIII, p. 182.

Bibliography

Whitman's Text:

Bradley, Sculley, and Stevenson, John, eds. *Walt Whitman's Backward Glances*. Philadelphia: University of Pennsylvania Press, 1947.

Bucke, R. M., Harned, T. B., and Traubel, H. L., eds. *The Complete Writings of Walt Whitman*, ten volumes. New York: G. P. Putnam's Sons, 1902.

Catel, Jean, ed. *The Eighteenth Presidency!* Paris: Tambour Edition, 1928.

Furness, Clifton J., ed. *Walt Whitman's Workshop*. Cambridge: Harvard University Press, 1928.

Gohdes, Clarence and Silver, Rollo G., eds. *Faint Clews & Indirections*. Durham: Duke University Press, 1949.

Holloway, Emory, ed. *The Uncollected Poetry and Prose of Walt Whitman*, two volumes. New York: Peter Smith, 1932.

Holloway, Emory and Adimari, Ralph, eds. *New York Dissected*. New York: Columbia University Press, 1936.

Holloway, Emory and Schwartz, Vernolian, eds. *I Sit and Look Out*. New York: Columbia University Press, 1932.

Kennedy, William Sloane, ed. *Walt Whitman's Diary in Canada*. Boston: Small, Maynard and Company, 1904.

Rodgers, Cleveland and Black, John, eds. *The Gathering of the Forces*, two volumes. New York: G. P. Putnam's Sons, 1920.

Rubin, Joseph J. and Brown, Charles H., eds. *Walt Whitman of the New York Aurora*. State College, Pennsylvania: Bald Eagle Press, 1950.

Traubel, Horace L., ed. *An American Primer*. Boston: Small, Maynard and Company, 1904.

Whitman, Walt. *Complete Prose Works*. Boston: Small, Maynard and Company, 1907.

Biographies:

Arvin, Newton. *Whitman*. New York: The Macmillan Company, 1938.

Bailey, John. *Walt Whitman*. New York: The Macmillan Company, 1926.

Barrus, Clara. *Whitman and Burroughs: Comrades*. New York: Houghton Mifflin Company, 1931.

Bazalgette, Leon. *Walt Whitman, The Man and His Work*. Translated by Ellen Fitzgerald. Garden City: Doubleday, Page and Company, 1920.

Binns, Henry Bryan. *A Life of Walt Whitman*. London: Methuen and Company, 1905.

Burroughs, John. *Whitman, A Study*. New York: Houghton Mifflin Company, 1896.

Canby, Henry Seidel. *Walt Whitman, An American*. New York: Houghton Mifflin Company, 1943.

Carpenter, Edward. *Days With Walt Whitman*. New York: The Macmillan Company, 1908.

Catel, Jean. *Walt Whitman, La Naissance Du Poete*. Paris: Les Editions Rieder, 1929.

Corbett, Elizabeth. *Walt: The Good Gray Poet Speaks for Himself*. New York: Frederick A. Stokes Company, 1928.

Donaldson, Thomas. *Walt Whitman, the Man*. New York: Francis P. Harper, 1896.

Faner, Robert D. *Walt Whitman & Opera*. Philadelphia: University of Pennsylvania Press, 1951.

Fausset, Hugh I'Anson. *Walt Whitman: Poet of Democracy*. New Haven: Yale University Press, 1942.

Glicksberg, Charles. *Walt Whitman and the Civil War*. Philadelphia: University of Pennsylvania Press, 1933.

[Hartmann], Sadakichi. *Conversations with Walt Whitman*. New York: E. P. Coby and Company, 1895.

Holloway, Emory. *Whitman, An Interpretation in Narrative*. New York: Alfred A. Knopf, 1926.

Irwin, Mabel MacCoy. *Whitman, The Poet-Liberator of Women*. New York: Privately printed, 1905.

Johnston, John and Wallace, J. W. *Visits to Walt Whitman in 1890-1891*. New York: Egmont Arens, 1918.

Keller, Elizabeth Leavitt. *Walt Whitman in Mickle Street*. New York: Mitchell Kennerley, 1921.

Kennedy, William Sloane. *Reminiscences of Walt Whitman*. London: Alexander Gardner, 1896.

Long, Haniel. *Walt Whitman and the Springs of Courage*. Santa Fe: Writer's Editions Inc., 1938.

Masters, Edgar Lee. *Whitman*. New York: Charles Scribner's Sons, 1937.

Morris, Harrison S. *Walt Whitman*. Cambridge: Harvard University Press, 1929.

O'Higgins, Harvey. *Alias Walt Whitman*. Newark: The Cateret Book Club, 1930.

Perry, Bliss. *Walt Whitman, His Life and Work*. New York: Houghton Mifflin Company, 1906.

Robertson, John. *Walt Whitman, Poet and Democrat*. Edinburgh: William Brown, 1884.

Rogers, Cameron. *The Magnificent Idler*. London: William Heinemann, Ltd., 1926.

Sawyer, Roland D. *Walt Whitman, The Prophet-Poet*. Boston: The Gorham Press, 1913.

Schyberg, Frederik. *Walt Whitman.* Translated by Evie Allison Allen. New York: Columbia University Press, 1951.

Selincourt, Basil de. *Walt Whitman, A Critical Study.* New York: Mitchell Kennerley, 1914.

Shephard, Esther. *Walt Whitman's Pose.* New York: Harcourt, Brace and Company, 1936.

Symonds, John A. *Walt Whitman, A Study.* London: John C. Nimmo, 1893.

Thomson, James. *Walt Whitman, The Man and the Poet.* London: Published by the Editor. 1910.

Traubel, Horace. *With Walt Whitman in Camden,* three volumes. New York: D. Appleton and Company, 1908.

Traubel, H. L., Bucke, R. M., and Harned, T. B., eds. *In Re Walt Whitman.* Philadelphia: David McKay, 1893.

Walling, William E. *Whitman and Traubel.* New York: Albert and Charles Boni, 1916.

Winwar, Frances. *American Giant, Walt Whitman and His Times.* New York: Harper and Brothers, 1941.

Other Works:

Canby, Henry Seidel. *American Estimates.* New York: Harcourt, Brace and Company, 1929.

Cargill, Oscar. *Intellectual America: Ideas on the March.* New York: The Macmillan Company, 1941.

Curti, Merle E. *The Growth of American Thought.* New York: Harper and Brothers, 1943.

Dowden, Edward. *Studies in Literature, 1789-1877.* London: C. Regan Paul and Company, 1878.

Ellis, Havelock. *The New Spirit.* London: Walter Scott, no date.

Foerster, Norman, ed. *The Reinterpretation of American Literature.* New York: Harcourt, Brace and Company, 1928.

Frank, Waldo. *The New America.* London: Jonathan Cape, 1922.

Gabriel, Ralph Henry. *The Course of American Democratic Thought.* New York: The Roland Press Company, 1940.

Gummere, Francis B. *Democracy and Poetry.* New York: Houghton Mifflin Company, 1911.

Jackson, Holbrook. *Dreamers of Dreams.* London: Faber and Faber Limited, 1948.

Matthiessen, P. O. *American Renaissance.* New York: Oxford University Press, 1941.

Mumford, Lewis. *The Golden Day.* New York: Boni and Liveright, 1926.

Nevinson, H. W. *Essays in Freedom and Rebellion.* New Haven: Yale University Press, 1921.

Parrington, Vernon Louis. *Main Currents in American Thought; an Interpretation of American Literature from the Beginnings to 1920.* New York: Harcourt, Brace and Company, 1930.

Rascoe, Burton. *Titans of Literature.* New York: G. P. Putnam's Sons, 1932.

Sherman, Stuart P. *Americans.* New York: Charles Scribner's Sons, 1924.

Van Doren, Carl C. *The Roving Critic.* New York: Alfred A. Knopf, 1923.

Vincent, Leon H. *American Literary Masters.* New York: Houghton Mifflin Company, 1906.

Westerfield, Hargis. *Walt Whitman's Reading.* Bloomington, Indiana: University Unpublished Doctoral Dissertation, 1949.

Articles:

Allen, Gay W. "Walt Whitman—Nationalist or Proletarian?" *English Journal,* Vol. XXVI (January, 1939), pp. 48-52.

Beatty, R. C. "Whitman's Political Thought." *South Atlantic Quarterly,* Vol. XLVI (1947), pp. 72-83.

Bozard, J. F. "Horace Traubel's Socialistic Interpretations of Whitman." *Furman Bulletin,* Vol. XX (January, 1938), pp. 35-45.

Bradley, Sculley. "Walt Whitman and the Post-War World." *South Atlantic Quarterly,* Vol. XLII (July, 1943), pp. 220-224.

Canby, H. S. "Who Speaks for New World Democracy." *Saturday Review of Literature,* Vol. XXVI (January 16, 1943), pp. 3-4, 16-18.

Cooke, Alice L. "Whitman's Background in the Industrial Movements of His Time." Studies in English, number 14, *University of Texas Bulletin* (July 8, 1936), pp. 124-137.

Cowley, Malcolm. "Whitman: The Philosopher." *New Republic,* Vol. CXVII (September 29, 1947), pp. 29-31.

———. "Whitman: The Poet." *New Republic,* Vol. CXVII (October 20, 1947), pp. 27-30.

Curti, Merle E. "Walt Whitman, Critic of America." *Sewanee Review,* Vol. XXXVI (April-June, 1928), pp. 130-138.

Ely, Catherine Beach. "Whitman and the Radicals as Poets of Democracy." *The Open Court,* Vol. XXXVI (October, 1922), pp. 594-601.

Finkel, W. L. "Walt Whitman's Manuscript Notes on Oratory." *American Literature,* Vol. XXII (March, 1950), pp. 29-52.

Furness, C. J. "Walt Whitman's Politics." *American Mercury,* Vol. XVI (April, 1929), pp. 459-466.

Holloway, Emory. "Whitman As Critic of America." *Studies in Philology,* Vol. XX (July, 1923), pp. 345-369.

———. "Whitman As A Journalist." *Saturday Review of Literature,* Vol. VIII (April 23, 1932), pp. 679-680.

Lessing, O. E. "Walt Whitman's Message." *The Open Court,* Vol. XXXIII (August, 1919), pp. 449-462.

Myers, Henry Alonzo. "Whitman's Conception of the Spiritual Democracy, 1855-56." *American Literature,* Vol. VI (November, 1934), pp. 239-253.

Noguchi, Youe. "Whitmanism and Its Failure." *Bookman,* Vol. XLIX (March, 1919), pp. 95-97.

Paine, Gregory. "Literary Relations of Whitman and Carlyle with Especial Reference to their Contrasting Views on Democracy." *Studies in Philology,* Vol. XXXVI (July, 1939), pp. 550-563.

Rodgers, Cleveland. "Walt Whitman the Poet of Democracy." *Mentor,* Vol. XI (September, 1923), pp. 3-14.

Rubin, J. S. "Whitman and Carlyle." *Modern Language Notes,* Vol. LIII (May, 1938), pp. 370-371.

Stewart, G. R. "Whitman and His Own Country." *Sewanee Review,* Vol. XXXIII (April, 1925), pp. 210-218.

Stovall, Floyd. "Main Drifts in Whitman's Poetry." *American Literature,* Vol. IV (March, 1923), pp. 3-21.

Van Doren, Mark. "Walt Whitman, Stranger." *American Mercury,* Vol. XXXV (July, 1925), pp. 277-285.

Wood, James N. "Democratic Vistas." *The Open Court,* Vol. XXXVI (October, 1922), pp. 575-585.

History:

Bogart, Ernest L. and Kemmerer, Donald L. *Economic History of the American People.* New York: Longmans, Green and Company, 1942.

Destler, Chester M. *American Radicalism, 1865-1901.* New London: Connecticut College, 1946.

Dorfman, Joseph. *The Economic Mind in American Civilization, 1606-1865.* New York: The Viking Press, 1946.

Faulkner, Harold U. *American Economic History.* New York: Harper and Brothers, 1938.

————. *American Political and Social History,* New York: F. S. Crofts and Company, 1943.

Gettell, Raymond G. *History of American Political Thought.* New York: D. Appleton-Century Company, 1928.

Hockett, Homer C. *Political and Social Growth of the American People, 1492-1865.* New York: The Macmillan Company, 1940.

Kirkland, Edward C. *A History of American Economic Life.* New York: F. S. Crofts and Company, 1932.

MacDonald, William. *Jacksonian Democracy, 1829-1837.* New York: Harper and Brothers, 1906.

Schlesinger, Jr., Arthur M. *The Age of Jackson.* Boston: Little, Brown and Company, 1947.

Schlesinger, Jr., Arthur M. *Political and Social Growth of the United States, 1852-1933.* New York: The Macmillan Company, 1935.

INDEX